W9-CMO-777

This is the first full-length study of five US banking panics of the Great Depression. Previous studies of the Depression have approached the banking panics from a macroeconomic viewpoint; Professor Wicker fills a lacuna in current knowledge by reconstructing a close historical narrative of each of the panics, investigating their origins, magnitude, and effects. He makes a detailed analysis of the geographical incidence of the disturbances using the Federal Reserve District as the basic unit, and reappraises the role of Federal Reserve officials in the panics. His findings challenge many of the commonly held assumptions about the events of 1930 and 1931, for example the belief that the increase in the discount rate in October 1931 initiated a wave of bank suspensions and hoarding. This meticulous account will be of wide interest to students of the Great Depression, monetary and financial historians, financial economists and macroeconomists.

Studies in Monetary and Financial History

Editors: Michael Bordo and Forrest Capie

The banking panics of the Great Depression

The banking panics of
the Great Depression

ELMUS WICKER

Indiana University

CAMBRIDGE
UNIVERSITY PRESS

WITHDRAWN
SCCCC - LIBRARY
4601 Mid Rivers Mall Drive
St. Peters, MO 63376

Published by the Press Syndicate of the University of Cambridge
The Pitt Building, Trumpington Street, Cambridge CB2 1RP
40 West 20th Street, New York, NY 10011–4211, USA
10 Stamford Road, Oakleigh, Melbourne 3166, Australia

© Cambridge University Press 1996

First published 1996

Transferred to digital printing 1998

Printed in Great Britain by Biddles Short Run Books

A catalogue record for this book is available from the British Library

Library of Congress cataloguing in publication data
Wicker, Elmus.
The banking panics of the Great Depression / Elmus Wicker.
    p.   cm. – (Studies in monetary and financial history)
Includes bibliographical references and index.
ISBN 0 521 56261 9 (hc)
1. Banks and banking – United States – History – 20th century.
2. Bank failures – United States – History – 20th century.
3. Financial crises – United States – History – 20th century.
4. Depressions – 1929 – United States.
5. United States – Economic conditions – 1918–1945.
I. Title.   II. Series.
HG2481.W493   1996
332.1′0973′09043–dc20   95–49436   CIP

ISBN 0 521 56261 9

CE

To my parents

"But the first duty of an economist is to describe correctly what is out there: a valid description without a deeper explanation is worth a thousand times more than a clever explanation of nonexistent facts."

Paul Samuelson, *Papers*, p. 1543

Contents

Figures

Tables

Preface

More than nine thousand banks failed in the United States between 1930 and 1933 equal to some 30 percent of the total number of banks in existence at the end of 1929. This clearly represents the highest concentration of bank suspensions in the nation's history. The rate of increase of bank suspensions was discontinuous. The data reveal at least four separate intervals when there was a marked acceleration and then deceleration in the number of bank failures: November 1930 to January 1931, April to August 1931, September and October 1931, and February and March 1933. Friedman and Schwartz (1963) designated these four episodes as banking panics to which special macroeconomic significance was attached. If we exclude the 3,400 banks that were not licensed by the Secretary of the Treasury to reopen at the end of the Banking Holiday in March 1933 only two out of five bank suspensions occurred during banking panics. It is well to bear in mind that 60 percent of bank closings between 1930 and 1932 were not panic induced, and that the problem of understanding why so many banks failed during the Great Depression goes beyond simply explaining what happened during banking panics although the evidence is conflicting whether the causes of individual bank suspensions differ between panic and nonpanic periods.

Nevertheless, banking panics represent a class of economic disturbance whose origin is to be found in an abrupt and unanticipated revision of expectations whose effects may be correctly described as traumatic. These disturbances include stock market manias and hyperinflations as well. In fact, there is something to be said for studying these phenomena as a subdiscipline and labelling it traumatic economics! The extent of the trauma however cannot be assumed; it must be demonstrated.

A banking panic may be defined as a class of economic shocks whose origin can be found in any sudden and unanticipated revision of expectations of deposit loss where there is an attempt to substitute currency for checkable deposits. In the past banking panics were regarded as examples of irrational or inscrutable behavior, but more recently they have been treated as rational depositor responses to an asymmetric information deficit. Depositors do not have access to the same information as do the banks on the quality of the bank's loan portfolio. The revival of interest in theories of banking panics has inevitably generated a renewal of interest in the history of particular banking panics as a partial test of the validity of rival theories.

But my own interest in banking panics goes back at least thirty years when I first began to study Federal Reserve monetary policy. At that time my attention was focused, among other things, on the response of Reserve officials to the banking crises of the Great Depression. Fifteen years elapsed, however, before I was able to have a closer look at the first of the four banking crises of the Great Depression. In two separate papers (1980, 1982) I reconsidered the causes and the expenditure effects of the 1930 banking crisis. The first paper would not have been possible had I not discovered quite by accident while browsing in the library John McFerrin's (1939[1969]) remarkable but largely neglected study of Caldwell and Company, the largest investment banking house in the South and whose collapse initiated a run on at least 120 banks in four states in November. McFerrin through meticulous scholarship traced the course of the panic and assessed the quality of Caldwell's management. The role of Caldwell and Company in generating the November panic had been described briefly by Raymond Goldschmidt (1933). But it was McFerrin who reconstructed the banking crisis following Caldwell's demise. I know of no other study of US financial panics of comparable scope and historical detail. It is a classic whose significance cannot be overestimated. McFerrin's work provided the basis for my reexamination of the 1930 crisis.

My research interest on banking crises of the Great Depression languished for ten years while I pursued other concerns, but it was rekindled by two considerations: (1) I discovered how little was known about the banking panic that followed Britain's departure from the gold standard in September 1931, and (2) Calomiris and Gorton's (1991) conjecture that the banking crises of the Great Depression did not resemble pre-1914 banking panics.

Apart from some general macroeconomic references to the September–October 1931 panic by Friedman and Schwartz nothing was available at the microeconomic level that described either the geographical incidence of the crisis or the names and locations of the failed banks in those areas. I had to reconstruct the panic from old newspaper files and Federal Reserve data on currency hoarding as revealed in the weekly balance sheets of the twelve Federal Reserve banks.

Calomiris and Gorton attempted to explain the relevance of the rival theories of banking panics to understanding pre-1914 experience. In passing, and almost as an afterthought, they proferred the suggestion that the banking crises of the Great Depression did not resemble pre-1914 banking panics. The time was ripe, I thought, for a reexamination of all four banking crises of the Great Depression. That meant undertaking separate studies of the second banking crisis from April to August 1931 and the Banking Panic of 1933. From these separate studies in addition to the previous two (November 1930–January 1931 and September–October 1931) this book has emerged.

Reconstructing the banking crises of the Great Depression has been a source of special archival difficulties. Pre-1914 banking panics had their origins in the New York money market, and a description of what happened was mainly an account of events taking place in that market. Hence, New York City newspapers are our primary source materials for the microhistory of the various panics. Sprague's (1910) famous history of crises under the national banking system relied heavily on local newspaper accounts of events in the New York money market. But bank suspensions in the interior were not given similar treatment because of the difficulty of obtaining detailed information on the closure of interior urban and rural banks. Therefore, we know relatively little about the diffusion of banking panics to the interior and the incidence of panics in particular cities and rural areas.

The New York money market did not play a similar role during the banking crises of the Great Depression, and a description of what happened in that market does not capture what was going on in the rest of the country. Although Friedman and Schwartz assigned a causal role to the failure of the Bank of United States in New York City in December 1930, the origin of the 1930 panic predates its collapse. And the coverage of what was happening in the interior by New York newspapers was not always satisfactory. To describe the course of the banking crises of the Great Depression an extensive search was undertaken of old newspaper files in the cities of Detroit, Philadelphia, Pittsburgh, Chicago, Cleveland, and Toledo as well as New York City.

Because newspaper editors were conscious of their responsibilities not to exacerbate banking disturbances, their description of what was happening was held to a not very informative minimum. Rarely, for example, do we learn whether or not a bank closure was the result of a bank run or some other cause. Granted that the information available may leave something to be desired, the best that we can do is to strive to get the story straight even if there are some significant details still missing.

I am grateful to those who have read an individual chapter or chapters and made suggestions for improvement: Michael Bordo, Charles Calomiris, Anna Schwartz, David Wheelock, Eugene White, Barrie Wigmore, Bill Witte; and Sandy Hanson seasonally adjusted Federal Reserve notes in circulation by individual Federal Reserve Districts. To my colleagues in the workshop in Economic History, I owe a debt of gratitude that has grown enormously over the years: George Alter, Jim Riley, and Elyce Rotella. They have acted as a sounding board for my ideas more times than they would care to remember.

1 The banking situation in the United States, 1921–33

The dimensions of the bank failure problem are clearly revealed in the data on bank suspensions. The total number of commercial banks in the US was reduced by one-half between 1921 and 1933. This drastic shrinkage in the number of independent banks represents the single most important development in the banking industry in the interwar period. A grand total of 15,348 banks were either suspended or merged with other banks. Of that number 14,808 suspended operations, 5,712 of which closed between 1921 and 1929 (39 percent) and 9,096 (61 percent) between 1930 and 1933. As we can see from table 1.1, bank failures were a recurring feature of the post-World War 1 financial landscape.

Banking failures between 1921 and 1929 were not panic related; this was a relatively panic-free period when bank suspensions had no effect on general depositor confidence as measured by an increase in currency in circulation. Between 1930 and 1932 of the more than 5,000 banks that closed only 38 percent suspended during the first three banking crisis episodes. Banking crisis episodes are identifiable in only ten of the thirty-six months: November 1930 to January 1931, April to August 1931, and September and October 1931. The percentage of banks failing in panic designated months was forty-five in 1930, fifty-seven in 1931 and zero in 1932. Over 60 percent of bank closings occurred in nonpanic months.

That is not to say that the ending of a banking crisis episode did not leave a residue of increased hoarding, eroded depositor confidence, and falling security prices that affected bank solvency in subsequent periods. The distinction between panic and nonpanic-related suspensions loses its sharpness in 1931 and 1932. But the distinction holds unequivocally for 1930. Bank suspensions during the first ten months of 1930 could not have been panic related since the onset of the first banking crisis was November.

The fourth banking panic in February and March 1933 did not resemble the three previous crises of the Great Depression. The panic did not manifest itself in individual bank suspensions. In February and

1

Table 1.1 *Total number and deposits of commercial banks and number and deposits of suspended banks, 1921–33*

Year	Total number of banks	Total deposits of banks $m.	Number of suspended banks	Deposits of suspended banks $m.	Failed banks as % of total banks[a]	Deposits of suspended banks as % of total deposits[a]
1921	29,788*	38,505*	505	172	0.31	0.24
1922	29,458*	40,814*	366	91	0.51	0.37
1923	28,877	45,893	646	150	0.73	0.46
1924	28,185	50,888	775	210	0.60	0.33
1925	27,638	54,111	618	168	0.94	0.48
1926	26,751	54,581	976	260	0.74	0.36
1927	25,800	57,622	669	199	0.55	0.25
1928	24,968	61,480	498	142	0.93	0.38
1929	24,026	59,832	659	231	3.48	1.40
1930	22,172	58,092	1,350	837	7.62	2.87
1931	19,375	49,509	2,293	1,690	3.64	1.43
1932	17,802	45,886	1,453	706	20.2	7.84
1933	14,440	42,125	4,000	3,597		

Notes: * Data only for June 30. Data for 1923–33 for December 31.

[a] Number of failed banks or deposits of suspended banks as a percentage of total number of banks and total deposits at the beginning of year. Total number of banks at beginning of 1922 = number of banks on December 31, 1921.

Source: Data on total number of banks and total deposits of commercial banks: Board of Governors of the Federal Reserve System, *Banking and Monetary Statistics: 1914–1941*, Washington DC, August 1976, pp. 16–17.

Data on Number of bank suspensions and deposits of suspended banks, Board of Governors of the Federal Reserve System, *Federal Reserve Bulletin*, September 1937, pp. 907 and 909.

March a sequence of bank moratoria or bank holidays were declared by the governors of the several states effectively restricting deposit withdrawals. On March 4 bank moratoria were in effect in all forty-eight states. President Roosevelt simply acknowledged a *fait accompli* by declaring a national banking holiday for March 6 through March 13. When some banks were allowed to reopen on March 13, there was a return of depositor confidence for the first time since the onset of the first banking panic in 1930 as evidenced by a massive return flow of currency to the banks. Three thousand and four hundred banks were not licensed to reopen after the banking holiday. However, if we include the 3,400 banks that were not allowed to reopen in the bank failure total, the proportion of bank suspensions during panic episodes rises to two-thirds during the Great Depression. It is primarily to these panic episodes to which our study is directed rather than to all of the bank failures of the depression years.

States of the economy: 1921–9 and 1930–3:

The backdrop to this record of bank suspensions was an interval of sustained real economic expansion from 1921 to 1929, at an annual rate between 5 and 6 percent and an average unemployment percentage between 4.6 and 5.5 percent depending on whose set of estimates we use (see table 1.2). This was followed by a shorter period of severe economic contraction from 1929 to 1933. But recent revision of both unemployment and real GNP estimates by Romer (1986, 1989) and by Balke and Gordon (1989) show output increasing in both sets of recession years – 1923–4 and 1926–7. Romer's new unemployment estimates reveal a much milder rate of unemployment increase – a one percentage point increase between 1923 and 1924 and a 0.52 percentage point increase between 1926 and 1927. Bank suspensions in the 1920s occurred when there were no serious disturbances to output and employment, and there were no national banking panics. Prices were relatively stable.

Agriculture, however, did not share in the general prosperity of the twenties. During World War 1 agricultural output had expanded rapidly and was attended by a rise in farm prices. The expansion was not sustainable once peace had been restored. Farm prices fell by more than 40 percent during the short depression in 1920–1; they never fully recovered in the 1920s. The real value of farm mortgage debt escalated. The troubled state of agriculture affected many small rural banks that had greatly increased in numbers during and immediately after the war. Burdened by illiquid farm debt and with no prospect for asset diversification, many of these banks were forced to close.

Table 1.2 *Real GNP, unemployment percentage, and implicit GNP deflator, 1921–33*

Year	Real GNP 1982 $ Commerce Dept.	Real GNP 1982 $ Romer	Unemployment percentage historical statistics	Unemployment percentage Romer	GNP implicit price deflator 1982 = 100
1921	452.8	486.4	11.7	8.7	15.0
1922	519.6	514.9	6.7	6.93	14.3
1923	576.9	583.1	2.4	4.8	14.6
1924	582.7	600.4	5.0	5.8	14.5
1925	625.0	615.1	3.2	4.92	14.7
1926	662.3	655.0	1.8	4.05	14.7
1927	661.2	661.4	3.3	4.57	14.5
1928	667.7	669.3	1.2	5.02	14.6
1929	709.6	709.6	3.2	4.61	14.6
1930	642.8		8.9	8.94	14.0
1931	588.1		16.3		12.4
1932	509.2		24.1		11.2
1933	498.5		25.2		11.0

Source: Christina D. Romer, "World War I and the Post-War Depression: A Reinterpretation Based on Alternative Estimates of GNP," *Journal of Monetary Economics*, 22 (July 1988), p. 106.
Christina D. Romer, "Spurious Volatility in Historical Unemployment Data," *Journal of Political Economy*, 94 (February 1986), p. 31.

Economic expansion came to an end in 1929 and was followed by the most severe contraction in US history. Real GNP fell by almost 30 percent between 1929 and 1932; unemployment reached 25 percent of the labor force, and the average price level of output declined by 23 percent. The precipitous decline in output and employment was accompanied by a sequence of bank suspensions that accelerated and decelerated with recurring frequency especially in 1930 and 1931. Friedman and Schwartz (1963) have identified four separate episodes of accelerated bank suspensions and labelled them banking crises or banking panics. This record of financial turmoil had no historical precedent. Single banking panics had occurred during the contraction phase of the cycle in 1884, 1890, 1893, and 1907. But the 1929–33 contraction was unique in the annals of banking panics in as much as it was interlaced with four distinct banking disturbances.

Although to accompany does not imply to cause, the close association of a decline in output with increased bank suspensions raises the puzzling question of the direction of causality. Conceivably, banking failures may have been the passive consequence of declining income and prices – an endogenous response. Or, they might have been a purely autonomous response to an unanticipated shock to depositor confidence – an exogenous response. Our study of the banking crises of the Great Depression should shed some light on this important question.

Although the bank failure experience of the twenties contrasts sharply with that of the early thirties, the latter experience cannot be fully appreciated without some knowledge of the former.

The incidence of bank suspensions

Bank suspensions were far more numerous in the twenties than they had been in any decade between 1890 and 1920. Between 1892 and 1899, the bank suspension rate averaged ninety per year; between 1900 and 1909 it was forty-nine a year and between 1910 and 1919 sixty-six a year. However, between 1921 and 1929 an average of more than 600 banks failed annually, a little less than ten times the annual average in the previous decade with average annual deposits in suspended banks of $180 million. The year 1926 was especially bad. Over 970 banks closed with $250 million of total deposits. Contributing to the high failure rate was an unusually severe banking panic in Florida and Georgia in June when 115 banks in the Manley–Anthony banking chain suspended with $30 million of depositor losses (Vickers, 1994, p. 5). Bank failures of the twenties were not accompanied by a general loss of depositor confidence as measured by the behavior of hoarding. There were no banking panics of national significance, and no disturbances in the New York money market.

The contemporary explanation for the high failure rate was an excessive number of banks in rural areas due to an unusually rapid rate of expansion between 1900 and 1920. These areas were said to be "overbanked," but what this meant was never carefully defined. Who was to say what the criteria ought to be for determining the right number of banks? The market provided a clear answer, but bank regulators were not willing to accept the verdict of the market. An area was overbanked when there were more banks than the regulators regarded as desirable!

There was also some recognition that the market structure of banking in the US contributed to the high failure rate. Bank chartering authority was shared by the Federal government and the individual states as well as the regulation of banking. The proliferation of a large number of small unit banks especially in agricultural areas increased the susceptibility of these banks to failure when confronted by any external shock.

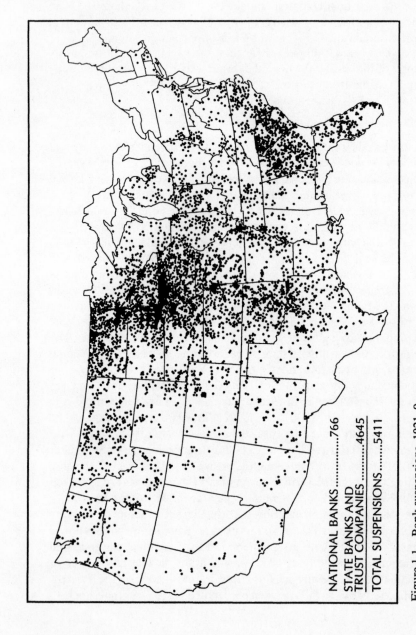

NATIONAL BANKS............766

STATE BANKS AND
TRUST COMPANIES..........4645

TOTAL SUSPENSIONS.......5411

Figure 1.1   Bank suspensions, 1921–9
Source: Board of Governors of the Federal Reserve System. *Bank Suspensions in the United States, 1892–1931,*
Vol. 5, Washington, D.C., 1933.

Seventy percent of all bank suspensions were located in twelve agricultural states (see figure 1.1) including seven Western states (Minnesota, North and South Dakota, Iowa, Nebraska, Missouri, and Kansas) plus Georgia, South Carolina, Montana, Oklahoma, and Texas whereas in 1930 and 1931 only 40 percent of bank suspensions occurred in those same states.

Bank suspensions in the twenties were concentrated in predominantly rural agricultural regions of the Midwest and Southeastern states where the typical bank was small. Four-fifths of all bank failures were located in places with fewer than 2,500 inhabitants. Sixty percent of the closed banks were banks with a capital stock of $25,000 or less. Only 20 per cent of the loans and investments of suspended banks were in cities with a population of 25,000 or more. Failures were more numerous where the number of banks showed the greatest increase prior to 1920. And where population per bank was the smallest in 1920.

The geographical incidence of bank failures shifted in 1930 and 1931 to Tennessee, Kentucky, Arkansas, North Carolina, Pennsylvania, and Ohio. Bank suspensions in both periods were mainly in rural communities. Over 75 percent of all bank suspensions between 1921 and 1929 were banks that were not members of the Federal Reserve System. Although deposits of nonmember suspended banks accounted for two-thirds of the deposits of closed banks, nonmember banks accounted for a little less than one quarter of total deposits of all commercial banks.

Banking failures during the 1920s apparently had a negligible effect on the growth of deposits and banking assets. Such a high failure rate may have led to some depositor inconvenience, but the macroeconomic consequences were minimal.

Bank suspensions in both periods were largely, as we have stated, in rural communities. But the percentage of bank suspensions in towns of fewer than 2,500 declined from 79 percent between 1921 and 1929 to 68 percent between 1930 and 1932. The percentage, though small, of bank suspensions in places where the population was greater than 25,000 nearly doubled – from 6.5 percent in the former period to 11.7 percent in the latter. Urban failures played a distinctively more prominent role during the Great Depression than they had during the 1920s.

Years that encompass the first three banking crises (1930–2) show a marked shift in the number of suspensions and deposits in failed banks from nonmember to member banks. Deposits in nonmember failed banks dropped from 75 percent in 1929 to 62 percent in 1932. Between January and March 1933, the shift was even more striking. The deposit share of nonmember suspended banks fell to 33 percent reflecting the fact that an overwhelmingly large amount of deposits in failed banks originated with member banks who were not licensed to reopen; these banks did not voluntarily suspend operations and, therefore, deserve to be treated separately from the bank closings before the onset of the state and national bank moratoria.

Financial condition of US banks: 1921–9 and 1930–3

The financial condition of US banks, one might have thought, should be the harbinger of the relatively high bank failure rate between 1921 and 1933. This is indeed the case during the Great Depression. Nevertheless, we have been unable to uncover any measures of performance for certain broad classifications of banks – national and state, nonmember and member, reserve city and country – that revealed financial weaknesses in the twenties. Earnings and profits as well as various measures of rates of return show a healthy and robust banking industry. Only by disaggregating the data by geographical region for national banks were we able to identify a disproportionate number of "weak" banks in some regions rather than others. These regions also happened to be areas where the bank failure rate was the highest in the 1920s.

Table 1.3 shows gross and net earnings and net profits also expressed as a percentage of total assets for member banks 1919–39. Dollar amounts of earnings and net profits display a strong cyclical response. During the twenties total assets increased by more than 50 percent; net earnings grew by 34 percent and net profits by 90 percent. Net profits practically evaporated in 1931 and became strongly negative in 1932 and 1933. Rate of return measures of bank profitability in the twenties also reveal a healthy financial condition of the banks. A preferred measure of bank profitability is the ratio of net profits to capital accounts. Since commercial banks compete with other businesses for capital, investors will compare rates of return in banking to rates of return in other industries. Net profits as a percentage of capital is set out in table 1.3 for member banks. The rate of return averaged 7.4 percent for member banks in the 1920s. The rate of return on capital for national banks was only slightly higher at 7.6 percent. This compares favorably with the 8.5 percent return on capital for national banks in the relatively failure-free period between 1941 and 1961. It averaged −3.1 percent for national banks and −1.75 percent for member banks between 1930 and 1933.

An alternative measure of bank profitability is net profits as a percentage of total assets. The rate of return on total assets increased from 0.94 in 1921 to a high of 1.17 in 1929. By way of comparison, it was only 0.68 in

Table 1.3 *Earnings and profits of member banks, 1919–39*[a]

Calendar year	In millions of dollars				As percentages of total assets			Net profits as a percentage of capital accounts
	Gross earnings[b]	Net earnings[b]	Net profits	Total assets[c]	Gross earnings[b]	Net earnings[b]	Net profits	
1919	1,436	455	351	29,770	4.83	1.53	1.18	
1920	1,804	577	396	32,374	5.57	1.78	1.22	10.2
1921	1,744	534	293	31,278	5.58	1.71	0.94	7.1
1922	1,652	506	349	31,414	5.26	1.61	1.11	8.3
1923	1,720	487	337	34,099	5.04	1.43	0.99	7.7
1924	1,763	498	356	36,385	4.91	1.39	0.99	8.1
1925	1,919	551	420	39,304	4.88	1.40	1.07	9.0
1926	2,028	586	432	41,094	4.94	1.43	1.05	8.9
1927	2,014	498	447	42,800	4.71	1.16	1.05	5.8
1928	2,194	580	504	45,596	4.81	1.27	1.11	5.6
1929	2,399	715	557	47,533	5.05	1.51	1.17	6.1
1930	2,158	554	307	47,164	4.58	1.17	0.65	4.6
1931	1,841	506	12	43,991	4.19	1.15	0.03	0.19
1932	1,554	410	−255	37,042	4.19	1.11	−0.69	−4.5
1933	1,237	378	−356	34,367	3.71	1.13	−1.07	−7.3
1934	1,244	394	−225	37,176	3.35	1.06	−0.61	−4.5
1935	1,207	374	212	41,613	2.90	0.90	0.51	
1936	1,271	399	465	45,904	2.77	0.87	1.01	

Table 1.3 (*Cont.*)

Calendar year	In millions of dollars				As percentages of total assets			
	Gross earnings[b]	Net earnings[b]	Net profits	Total assets[c]	Gross earnings[b]	Net earnings[b]	Net profits	Net profits as a percentage of capital accounts
1937	1,321	419	337	47,510	2.78	0.88	0.71	
1938	1,274	384	265	47,434	2.69	0.81	0.56	
1939	1,296	401	347	52,129	2.49	0.77	0.68	

Notes: [a] Compiled from the Boatd of Governors of the Federal Reserve System, *Federal Reserve Bulletin* Annual Reports of the Comptroller of the Currency, and Board of Governors, *Banking Studies*, Baltimore, 1941, p. 437.
[b] Through 1926 include profits on securities sold, which were thereafter treated as offsets to losses and charge-offs. The resulting inconsistency is not believed to be very great.
[c] Averages of assets reported by all member banks for each call date in the calendar year and the final call date in the preceding year, except that for 1933 only averages for the last three call dates in year were included.

Table 1.4 *Percentage of national banks grouped by geographical regions reporting net deficits or net profits of less than 3 percent of invested capital averaged for 1926–9 and 1930*

Geographical division	Average 1926–9 %	1930 %
Northeastern	10.75	42.0
Southeastern	22.00	37.2
North Central	21.20	42.6
Mid-continent	36.00	41.2
Western	31.80	34.9
Average all groups	24.40	40.6

Source: H. Parker Willis and John M. Chapman, *The Banking Situation*, New York, 1934, p. 166.

1962 for all commercial banks. There was a precipitous fall after 1929 to −1.07 in 1933 (see Figure 1.2)

There was nothing about the behavior of average rates of return, however measured, to portend their dramatic collapse after 1929. Average measures for each classification of banks may mask the extent of the variation among banks. Earnings and profit measures do not exist for many rural banks in areas with populations of less than 2,500, where bank failure rates were the highest. For these banks we should expect unfavorable earnings and net profits experience.

Banks in all geographical divisions of the country did not share the same net profit experience. Table 1.4 shows the percentage of national banks grouped by geographical region reporting net deficits or net profits of less than 3 percent of invested capital averaged for 1926–9 and separately for 1930. The agricultural difficulties of the twenties are reflected in the large proportion of banks of low profitability in the mid continent and Western states. We have also observed in figure 1.1 the high concentration of bank failures between 1921–9 in the mid continental region.

The ravages of the Great Depression contrast sharply with the experience of the 1920s. The percentage of national banks reporting net profits or net deficits of less than 3 percent of invested capital in 1930 quadrupled in the Northeastern region and doubled in the Southeastern and North Central regions. Total bank assets of member banks declined 30 percent; gross earnings fell 35 percent, and net earnings by 43 percent. And the most telling statistic of all – net profits almost evaporated in 1931 and became strongly negative in 1932, 1933, and 1934. The rate of

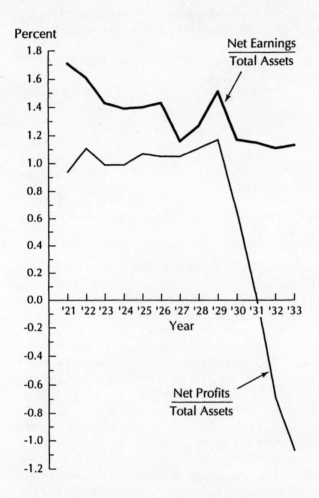

Figure 1.2   Rates of Return of Member Banks, 1921–33

return as measured by net profit to total assets ratio went to zero in 1931 and was negative during the next three years.

What is indeed surprising is how well the rate of return as measured by the net earnings to total asset ratio held up between 1930 and 1933 (figure 1.2) after the sharp drop in 1929. The explanation is to be found in the fact that the numerator of the ratio – net earnings – decreased less rapidly than the denominator – total assets – thus shoring up the ratio.

Table 1.5 *Losses on loans and investments per $100 of loans and investments and profits per $100 of capital funds for all member banks annually, 1929–32*

Year	Losses on loans per $100 of loans	Losses on investments per $100 of investment	Net profits per $100 of capital funds
1929	0.54	0.94	8.75
1930	0.78	1.05	4.56
1931	1.36	2.26	0.19
1932	2.41	2.59	−4.50

Source: Board of Governors of the Federal Reserve System, *Federal Reserve Bulletin*, June 1931, p. 394; July 1931, p. 424; and April 1934, p. 252.

Table 1.6 *Losses on loans and investments per $100 of loans and investments and net profits per $100 of capital funds for national and state member banks annually, 1929–32*

Year	National banks			State member banks		
	Loans losses per $100 of loans	Inv. loss per $100 of inv.	Net Profit per $100 Capital	Loans losses per $100 of loans	Inv. loss per $100 of inv.	Net profit per $100 capital
1929	0.62	0.94	7.77	0.43	0.95	10.16
1930	0.92	1.05	4.04	0.58	1.06	5.28
1931	1.62	2.47	−1.47	0.96	1.88	2.54
1932	2.49	2.51	−4.97	2.26	2.71	−3.84

Source: Board of Governors of the Federal Reserve System, *Federal Reserve Bulletin*: June 1931, p. 394; July 1931, p. 424; April 1934, p. 252.

Earnings experience alone does not warrant any inference about the bank suspension rate. Balance sheet data are also required on the amounts of bank capital and bank liquidity. But it is quite clear that earnings deficits weakened the banks, small as well as large, making them increasingly susceptible to collapse.

What is the explanation for the poor earnings and net profit performance between 1929 and 1933? The answer is to be found in the record of loan and investment losses per $100 of loans and investments for all member banks. Table 1.5 reveals the extent of the losses for all member banks. Losses per $100 of loans almost quintupled rising from 0.54 in 1929 to 2.41 in 1932.

Losses on investments exceeded loan losses per $100 of investments in every year. Net profits per $100 of capital funds were slashed from 8.75 in 1929 to −4.50 in 1932.

Table 1.6 breaks down loan and investment losses for national banks and for state chartered banks. Loan losses per $100 of loans were uniformly lower for state member banks. Investment losses were approximately the same in 1929 and 1930 but were lower for state member banks in 1931 and higher in 1932. Net profits per $100 of capital were higher for state member banks. The loan and investment loss record of member banks reflects the severity of the impact of the contraction on the banking industry as well as the distributional impact between national and state chartered banks.

Unfortunately, the complete story of the loan and investment loss record cannot be told, for we are missing essential data on the behavior of nonmember banks. At the end of 1929 nonmember banks constituted 63 percent of all commercial banks with a mere 22 percent of total deposit holdings. The proportion of nonmember banks had fallen to 57 percent and deposit share to 13 percent at the end of June 1933. We can only conjecture that the loan and investment loss record of nonmember banks would compare unfavorably with that of member banks both national and state chartered. But we cannot be certain. This is an area for future research. We do know, however, that there was a high concentration of loans and investments in suspended banks in places with populations of under 2,500 and that proportion fell between 1921–9 and 1930–2. Between 1921 and 1929 46 percent of the loans and investments were in suspended banks in places with under 2,500 people whereas in 1930–2 that ratio had fallen by more than one-half to 19 percent. In the twenties only 20 percent of loans and investments were in cities with populations over 25,000. That percentage had increased to fifty-seven between 1930 and 1932. The difference is even more striking in cities of 100,000 or greater. Loans and investments in closed banks were only 12 percent in 1920–9, but it had increased to 41 percent between 1930 and 1933.

Balance sheet data reveal that nonmember banks enjoyed fewer benefits from economic expansion and reaped a greater whirlwind from the Great Depression. Table 1.7 shows percentage changes in select balance sheet items for both member and nonmember banks for the two periods: June 30, 1921 to June 30, 1929 and June 30, 1929 to June 30, 1932. June call dates are used because no December dates are available prior to 1925. In the twenties nonmember banks did not share the same

Table 1.7 *Percentage change in select balance sheet items all member and nonmember banks between June 30, 1921–June 30, 1929 and June 30, 1929 and June 30, 1932*

	Percentage change June 30, 1921–June 30, 1929		Percentage change June 30, 1929 – June 30, 1932	
	Member*	Nonmember*	Member*	Nonmember*
Loans	42	27	−35	−48
Investments	68	70	14	−21
Government				
Securities	62	−5	36	−25
Other securities	71	116	−2	−20
Time deposits	54	37	−22	−42
Capital accounts	54	NA	−11	NA

Note: * June 30, call date. No December dates are available prior to 1925 for non-member banks.
Source: Board of Governors of the Federal Reserve System, *Banking and Monetary Statistics, 1914–1942*, Washington DC, 1976, pp. 22, 23, 72, and 74.

rate of expansion of deposits and loans as did member banks. Although the growth in investments was about the same, the composition of those investments was quite different. While member banks were expanding their government security portfolio by more than 60 percent, nonmembers were contracting their holdings of government securities by 5 percent. Nonmembers were shifting to less liquid securities. Other securities more than doubled. A riskier security portfolio meant greater vulnerability to financial shocks.

The burden of the economic contraction fell more heavily on the nonmember banks. Loans contracted by nearly one-half, and total deposits by 42 percent. Although total investments continued to expand for member banks (14 percent), they contracted by 21 percent for nonmember banks. Other securities decreased by $122 million for member banks and more than $500 million for nonmember banks. Sales of securities of that magnitude had seriously depressing effects on asset yield and asset prices. Considering the impact of the contraction on the balance sheet of nonmember banks, is it surprising that we observe a much higher incidence of bank insolvencies?

The decomposition of the loan and investment portfolios of all commercial banks should permit us to discern the principal differences, if any, among the various classifications of banks: member and nonmember, national and state, central reserve city, reserve city and country banks. Balance sheet data on call dates for all commercial banks including nonmember banks exist only for total loans with no separate breakdown by loan type. However, member bank data on call dates exist for three loan classifications: on securities, on real estate, and all other commercial from 1919 to 1933. For the period 1921–29 loans on securities doubled, lending on real estate increased 179 percent, and all other commercial remained unchanged. The percentage of real estate to total loans increased from 6.3 percent in 1921 to 12.6 percent in 1928 while the share of loans on securities rose from 18 percent to 26 percent. Between 1929 and 1932 loans on real estate declined by 10 percent and loans on securities by almost 50 percent. Nonfarm loans on real estate made up nearly 90 percent of the total real estate loans.

Real estate lending, primarily nonfarm, as we shall soon discover, was an important source of unsettled banking markets during the Great Depression. Banking unrest in Pittsburgh, Philadelphia, and especially Chicago was directly related to depreciated real estate values in 1931. Banks and Trust companies were the most vulnerable in outlying areas of each city.

The stage was set for the expansion of real estate lending by national banks after the passage of the McFadden-Pepper bill in 1927 which made limited provision for the purchase of real estate bonds by national banks and increased the aggregate amount of loans made by a national bank on real estate from one-third of time deposits to one-half as long as they did not exceed 25 percent of capital and surplus. Loans on real estate at national banks expanded more than 50 percent between 1927 and 1932 whereas real estate loans at state chartered banks expanded by only 3 percent. Real estate lending more than doubled at mutual savings banks, their share in the total having increased from 32 percent in 1927 to nearly 60 percent in 1932.

The increased sensitivity of national banks to depreciation of real estate values is revealed by real estate loans as a percentage of capital and surplus which increased from 24 percent in 1926 to 40 percent in 1927 to 57 percent by the end of 1932. It also reveals one important cause of the general illiquidity of national banks. The absence of statistics on the default rate on real estate loans, both farm and nonfarm, prevents any assessment of the risks involved in real estate lending.

A study conducted by the Federal Reserve including a sample of 105 closed banks in 1931 revealed that a number of the banks encountered difficulties because the banks either were operated by real estate promoters or exhibited excess enthusiasm to finance a local real estate boom. Excessive real estate lending in the twenties probably contributed to the increased illiquidity of American banks in the thirties.

Definitions, characteristics, and theories of banking panics

For the purpose of this study we define a banking panic to be an exogenous shock whose origins can be found in any sudden and unanticipated revision of expectations of deposit loss accompanied by an attempt to substitute currency for checkable deposits, a situation usually described as a run on the banks. A general loss of depositor confidence distinguishes a banking panic from other episodes of bank failures. A transfer of deposits from weak to strong banks during a bank run without any change in the public's preference for currency does not qualify.

Banking panics may be local, regional, or national in geographical incidence. However, that does not preclude economic effects from extending beyond local or regional boundaries. With the single exception of the 1893 panic, pre-1914 panics were restricted mainly to the New York money market with few bank suspensions in the rest of the country. Yet there were nonneglible national effects on the money stock and expenditures. Local and regional banking panics may not have had national effects. Whether they did or not must be looked for in each panic.

Friedman and Schwartz were the first to identify four separate national banking panics between 1930 and 1933. Each of the four crises had these distinguishing characteristics: (1) an increase in the number of bank failures; (2) an increase in the public's preference for currency in lieu of demand deposits; and (3) a decline in the stock of money. The decline in the stock of money presumably was what made the panic national in scope, not wide geographical diffusion of bank suspensions. But equally important, if not more important, were national expenditure effects. And Friedman and Schwartz postulated a causal link between changes in the money stock and expenditures.

We modify their list of distinguishing characteristics by substituting for (2) an increase in currency in circulation (hoarding) as proxied by Federal Reserve notes in circulation because the data are available both weekly and monthly. The loss of depositor confidence as reflected in an increase in Federal Reserve notes in circulation is in our judgment the key characteristic of a banking panic. And we add another characteristic feature of banking panics – an increase in deposits in failed banks. Our emphasis on the behavior of hoarding changes slightly the Friedman and Schwartz dating of some of the panic episodes. We also identify a fifth panic – a mini panic in the city of Chicago – in June 1932 which, if measured by the amount of hoarding, turns out to have been as significant as the first panic in 1930.

Analysis of the expenditure effects of the 1930 banking panic, and, perhaps, the second banking panic in 1931, have led us to conclude that at least two of the four banking panics identified by Friedman and Schwartz were region specific without any clearly identifiable national economic effects.

The word panic as conventionally used implies a theory of the origins of banking panics. The New Shorter Oxford Dictionary defines a panic as follows: "An excessive or unreasoning feeling of alarm or fear leading to extravagant or foolish behavior, such as that which may suddenly spread through a crowd of people." Past banking panics were regarded as prime examples of irrational conduct induced by a contagion of fear. This view of banking panics remained unquestioned until quite recently when an attempt was made to view banking panics as rational depositor responses to an asymmetric information deficit. Depositors do not have access to the same information as do the banks on the quality of the bank's loan portfolio.

Calomiris and Gorton (1991) identified for purely expository purposes two rival theories of banking panics around which, they maintain, research has "coalesced." One descends directly from the seminal work of Diamond and Dybvig (1983) and is labelled the random withdrawal hypothesis. The other has a varied origin including Chari and Jagannathan (1988), Gorton (1987), and Jacklin and Bhattacharya (1988) and is referred to as the asymmetric information approach. Calomiris and Gorton attempt to test the two theories as explanations of the pre-1914 banking panics. We go a step further and show the relevance of the two approaches to understanding the banking crises in 1930 and 1931.

Diamond and Dybvig show that par value deposits, that is, deposits fixed in price in terms of the unit of account, represent optimal bank contracts but lead to costly panics. They assign a specific role for banks to perform which is to transform illiquid assets into liquid liabilities for the explicit purpose of smoothing consumption. The issue of par value deposits presumably provides a better risk-sharing arrangement than is available in a competitive market. The sources of individual risk are not publicly observable, and a contingent market will fail to develop because private liquidity needs are unverifiable. These uninsured deposit contracts suffer from one major drawback, however, or so it is alleged. They subject banks to unanticipated deposit withdrawals, asset liquidation, and the threat of insolvency – clearly undesirable events.

The fundamental cause of banking panics is random withdrawals of currency among depositors who are subject to a first come, first serve rule determining the order of withdrawals. Exogenous currency withdrawals may produce contagion effects through a network of bank affiliated relationships. In the pre-1914 panics there were seasonal currency demand shocks generated by random withdrawals by interior banks. A run on a particular bank may be a sufficient signal to trigger a loss of depositor confidence which spreads to affiliated banks as well as to geographically contiguous banks.

The second approach to modelling banking panics was referred to as the asymmetric information approach by Calomiris and Gorton. Panics represent desired outcomes produced by a rational response to a change in beliefs about the riskiness of banks. The main source of a panic is an asset shock rather than an exogenous demand for currency. The panic is a device for resolving the problem of asymmetric information: loans are primarily nonmarketable bank assets, and depositors have no knowledge of the quality of these assets. Since depositors cannot distinguish individual bank risks Calomiris and Gorton (1991, p. 124) maintain "they may withdraw a large volume of deposits from all banks in response to a signal." Presumably, the weaker banks fail first. The relevance of the historical evidence to assessing the validity of the two rival theories will be explained in the concluding chapter.

Banking panics of the Great Depression: an overview

The banking situation on the eve of the Great Depression was better than at any time in the preceding ten years, except perhaps for small rural banks. Gross and net earnings as well as net profits were at an all time high. Although bank failures were higher than at any time since 1926, they were of purely local significance without implications at the national level. There were, nevertheless, some vulnerable spots, especially in those geographical regions where the bank suspension rate earlier had been the highest and among those banks that had heavily invested in real estate. During the first fifteen months of the contraction, the average number of bank suspensions was sixty-nine, not deserving of any more consideration than had been given to the closings in the mid-twenties.

In November and December 1930 the bank failure rate accelerated giving rise to the first of the four alleged national banking crises of the Great Depression. Both the November 1930–January 1931 and the January–March 1933 banking crises have received careful consideration elsewhere: Friedman and Schwartz (1963), Peter Temin (1976), Wicker (1980 and 1982), David Hamilton (1985), Susan Kennedy (1973), and Barrie Wigmore (1985). But the two 1931 banking crises have for some inexplicable reason escaped similar close scrutiny. This apparent lack of scholarly interest is difficult to reconcile with the startling fact that more banks failed in 1931 than in any other year in US history. Almost 2,300

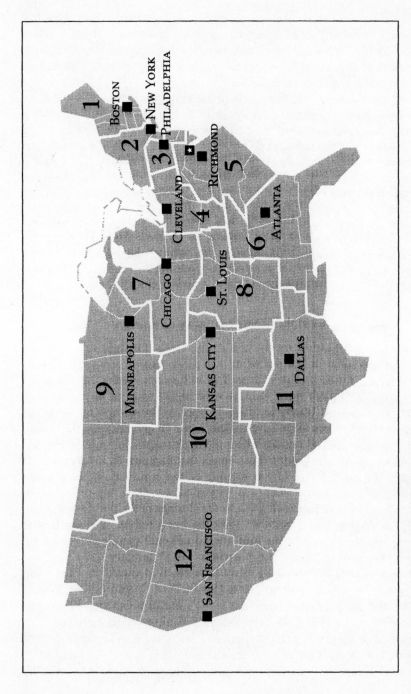

Figure 1.3   Map of the Federal Reserve system

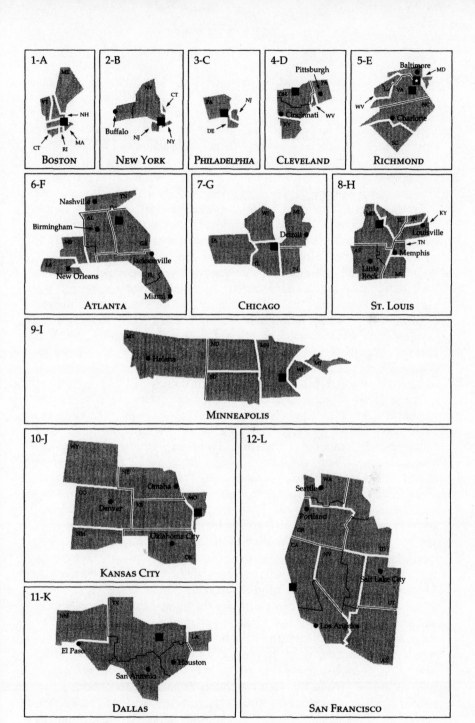

Figure 1.4   Map of the individual Federal Reserve Districts

banks failed with deposits of $1.7 billion. The number of bank suspensions represented 7.6 percent of all banking institutions in that year (table 1.1).

We propose to reconstruct each of the four banking crises in two separate stages. In the first, we employ as our basic unit of analysis each Federal Reserve District. In the second, we go a step further and attempt a microhistory of each crisis by identifying and describing banking disturbances in the geographical areas most affected. The selection of the Federal Reserve District as an appropriate geographical unit was not arbitrary. See figures 1.3 and 1.4 to identify the twelve Federal Reserve Districts. Data exist from which monthly estimates can be extracted for both the number of bank suspensions and deposits in suspended banks. What makes the selection of the Reserve District compelling is the availability of monthly data which we adjusted seasonally for the purpose of measuring changes in depositor confidence in different sections of the country. Changes in the amount of Federal Reserve notes in circulation serve as a useful proxy for depositor confidence in that District. We shall employ this measure of depositor confidence to distinguish between a region specific and a nationwide banking crisis and to map the geographical incidence of the crisis.

The analysis of geographical incidence has enabled us to locate the specific centers of banking disturbances in 1930 and 1931. The failure in November 1930 of the largest investment banking house in the South – Caldwell and Company of Nashville, Tennessee – accounts for the high concentration of bank suspensions within the St. Louis Federal Reserve District. And in 1931 bank suspensions in Toledo, Pittsburgh, Philadelphia, and Chicago explain the high concentration of suspensions, deposits in failed banks, and hoarding in the Cleveland, Philadelphia, and Chicago Districts. What are perhaps most conspicuous by their absence in 1930 and 1931 are crises in the New York money market. The banking panics of the Great Depression had their origin in the interior of the country with minimal repercussions in the central money market. This contrasts sharply with pre-1914 banking panics whose origins were in the New York money market where the impact on call money rates and the stock market was exceptionally severe, the single exception being the panic of 1893 whose origin was in the interior.

In 1933 the center of the banking crisis shifted to Detroit, but there were no runs on the banks and no bank failures, surely an anomalous state of affairs. When the Reconstruction Finance Corporation (RFC) refused to support two of Detroit's largest and weakest banks, the Governor of Michigan declared a statewide banking moratorium or banking holiday to prevent an imminent banking collapse. The closing of the Michigan banks spread fear and uncertainty to the contiguous states of Illinois, Indiana, and Ohio with an immediate impact on the Chicago and New York money markets as well. The response of each of the states was to initiate a bank moratorium or some form of deposit restriction scheme ending as it did with the declaration of a national banking holiday on March 6 by the newly inaugurated President Roosevelt. Preeminent among the unanswered questions is: Why was it necessary to resort to the pre-1914 device of the suspension of cash payments if the Fed had been created to make suspension obsolete?

A reappraisal of the Fed's responses to the banking crises may be called for in the light of new information uncovered in the banking panic narratives. For example, Fed officials successfully forestalled any panic in the New York money market; there were no spikes in the call money rate nor other short-term interest rates, and the monetary base increased. These responses are obviously pluses in the evaluation of Fed performance.

Their failure to have offset the increases in the currency–deposit ratio was understandable. Knowledge of the role of the currency–deposit ratio as a determinant of the money multiplier was not forthcoming before the pathbreaking contributions of Angell and Ficek in 1933 and James Meade in 1934. Furthermore, the narrative of events in September and October 1931 reveals that the acceleration of bank suspensions and hoarding were well under way before the Fed increased the discount rate. The increase in the discount rate in October 1931 did not cause the increase in bank closures and increased hoarding as is frequently alleged.

If the Fed can be faulted, it is for its failure to have attempted through open market operations to restore depositor confidence. Fed policymakers recognized that the ending of each of the first three banking panics did not lead to a return flow of currency to the banking system. A display of aggressive leadership by the Fed earlier on may have reversed the tide of ebbing depositor confidence and forestalled further bank suspensions. In the following three chapters we analyze in turn each of the banking crises of the Great Depression.

2 The banking crisis of 1930

The existence of a nationwide banking panic in November 1930 to January 1931 remains a matter of dispute. We can look in vain in the pages of the financial press for an event clearly designated as a banking panic; it was certainly not the name given to the accelerated bank suspensions in the final two months of 1930. The public had no difficulty in identifying the banking crises in 1873, 1884, 1893, and 1907. The passage of time should not have dulled the recognition of a banking crisis in 1930, especially if the events in those months bore a close resemblance to what had happened earlier.

Friedman and Schwartz (1963) were the first to characterize the accelaration of bank suspensions in November–January as a banking crisis or banking panic. They assigned a causal role to those bank failures to explain why the money stock fell and why the depression deepened, thereby giving dramatic emphasis to the significance of what had happened during those three months. The banking situation in 1930 took on a new relevance. But the primary concern of Friedman and Schwartz was macroeconomic; that is, they focused on the behavior of reserve and monetary aggregates and how they might have affected total output. They were only peripherally interested in the microhistory of the banking crisis except with respect to the failure of the Bank of United States in December. No mention was made of the failure of the Tennessee investment banking house of Caldwell and Co. in November, and no attempt was made to describe the geographical incidence of the banking crisis.

The task of describing what happened during the banking crisis remains incomplete. We still lack a detailed description of the geographical incidence of bank suspensions and hoarding. Our basic unit of observation is the Federal Reserve District. Data exist monthly for two bank failure measures: the number of bank suspensions and the amount of deposits in failed banks and two measures of currency hoarding, currency in circulation seasonally adjusted monthly and Federal Reserve notes in circulation by Federal Reserve District seasonally adjusted monthly. The high concentration of bank closings in only five of the twelve Federal Reserve Districts hardly testifies to the geographical dimensions of the banking crisis. There was no nationwide run on the banks in either November or December. Nor were the interest rate and expenditure effects of accelerated bank suspensions significant. We show that the Federal Reserve was successful in preventing a panic in the New York money market, a common occurrence in pre-1914 banking panics. However, they were less successful in restoring depositor confidence to pre-November levels even after the panic had subsided as evidenced by the absence of a return flow of hoarded currency (currency in excess of the normal seasonal inflow) in January 1931.

The first section describes the geographical incidence of the crisis; the second attempts to provide a microhistory of the banking disturbance; the expenditure effects of the crisis are analyzed in the fourth section; the fifth examines the 1930 crisis as a cause of the Great Depression; the sixth asks what was the role of the Federal Reserve; the seventh asks what should the Fed have done? And the final section consists of a short summary and conclusions.

1   The geographical incidence of the banking crisis of 1930

We begin by reviewing the record of bank suspensions, deposits in failed banks, and currency hoarding seasonally adjusted from the onset of the Great Depression in August 1929 to March 1931. Monthly data are set out in table 2.1. Although the number of bank suspensions and deposits in suspended banks increased perceptibly in November 1929 and January 1930 there was no banking panic. Nor was there an increase in hoarding defined as an increase in currency held by the public seasonally adjusted. A classic banking panic is triggered when households and business firms revise their expectations of future deposit losses. There is no evidence that depositors revised their expectations of deposit losses when the stock market collapsed in October 1929. Currency in circulation seasonally adjusted declined almost continuously from August 1929 to October 1930. Except for the increase in August 1930, currency held by the public seasonally adjusted behaved similarly. Considering pre-1914 banking crisis experience, it is indeed surprising that the external shock of the magnitude of the stock market collapse did not result in a banking panic. And the credit for this nonevent belongs to the Federal Reserve. In the aftermath of the collapse of the stock market, loans to the stock market were transferred smoothly to a few large New York City banks which, in the absence of Fed assistance, would have tightened the money market

Table 2.1 *Bank suspensions, deposits in closed banks($m.), and hoarding ($m.), monthly, August 1929–March 1931*

	Number of bank suspensions	Deposits in suspended banks	Curr. in circulation Seas. adj.* (Federal Reserve Board)	Curr. held by Public Seas. adj.* (Friedman and Schwartz)	Federal Reserve Notes in circulation seasonally adj. (Wicker)
1929					
August	18	7	4,525	3,919	1,862
September	37	10	4,500	3,822	1,869
October	41	12	4,465	3,832	1,844
November	70	22	4,475	3,852	1,886
December	61	15	4,435	3,800	1,820
1930					
January	90	27	4,385	3,752	1,746
February	87	32	4,335	3,748	1,692
March	80	23	4,305	3,717	1,644
April	90	32	4,275	3,670	1,588
May	59	19	4,270	3,694	1,536
June	68	69	4,255	3,681	1,482
July	64	30	4,240	3,669	1,410
August	67	23	4,225	3,704	1,370
September	67	22	4,180	3,634	1,366
October	72	25	4,155	3,594	1,359
November	256	180	4,155	3,674	1,357
December	352	372	4,315	3,809	1,484
1931					
January	198	76	4,425	3,818	1,521
February	77	35	4,370	3,823	1,484
March	86	34	4,355	3,861	1,486

Note: *average of daily figures.
Source: Board of Governors of the Federal Reserve System. *Banking and Monetary Statistics: 1914–1941*, Washington DC 1976, p.414.
Milton Friedman and Anna Schwartz, *A Monetary History of the United States 1867–1960*, Princeton,1963, pp. 712–13.
Board of Governors of the Federal Reserve System, *Annual Report of the Federal Reserve Board 1932*, p. 154.

and initiated a mad scramble for funds that might easily have precipitated a panic. This did not happen. On the day of the collapse (October 28) the Federal Reserve Bank of New York purchased $132 million of government securities without the prior approval of the Board in Washington and outside the Open Market Investment Committee's (OMIC) account. Between October 30 and November 20, the OMIC acquired securities at the rate of $25 million a week. Again on November 25 authorization was obtained for the purchase of an additional $200 million of securities. The New York Fed reduced its discount rate from 6 percent on November 1 to 4.5 percent on November 15. The Fed's immediate and effective response avoided a banking panic by endorsing a liberal discount policy combined with open market operations to ensure the orderly liquidation of stock market credit. This episode is especially revealing. The Fed demonstrated that it had learned the lesson of how to prevent banking crises whose origin was a shock to the central money market. As we intend to show, there was no panic in the central money market in each of the four banking crises of the Great Depression.

The first banking crisis of the Great Depression can be easily identified by the aggregate data in table 2.1. There was a sharp escalation in the number of bank suspensions and deposits in failed banks in both November and December 1930 and a deceleration in January with total deposit losses of $628 million. The deceleration in January is greater for deposits in failed banks than it is for the number of bank suspensions. Judged solely by deposits of failed banks, we might conclude that the panic was over by the end of December even though deposit losses remained three times greater in January than they had been in the previous October. Currency in circulation, however, is the more discriminating indicator of financial panic; it is a reliable measure, or better index, of the loss of depositor confidence in the banks. Currency held by the public seasonally adjusted increased by $224 million from October through January; likewise currency in circulation seasonally adjusted increased by $270 million during the same period. Federal Reserve Board data for currency in circulation show no change between October and November but a substantial change in December and January, whereas Friedman and Schwartz's estimates of currency held by the public increase in November and December and change very little in January. The discrepancy between the two estimates is probably attributable to the different techniques employed by the Federal Reserve Board and Friedman and Schwartz for seasonally adjusting the data. Data quirks aside, there is ample reason for considering January as the terminal month for the first banking crisis. Nevertheless, it is indeed significant to note that the ending of the crisis was not accompanied by an equivalent return flow of currency to the banks. Currency in circulation did not revert to its pre-crisis level, though it did decline in February and March. Currency held by the public did not decline at all. The increase in hoarding may have ended, but public confidence in the banking system had not been restored. Depositor confidence had been weakened thereby increasing depositor sensitivity to future unanticipated shocks.

The data on the number of bank suspensions, deposits in suspended banks, and currency hoarding provide criteria for identifying the duration of the crisis as well as measures of its magnitude and severity. The aggregate data can tell us what happened but not where it happened; they cannot tell us whether or not the crisis was region specific or fully national in scope. For that we must seek the help of microhistory. We ought to be able to map the geographical incidence of the banking crisis and provide a complete narrative of the sequence of events associated with bank suspensions in specific Federal Reserve Districts.

Table 2.2 sets out the data for bank suspensions and deposits in failed banks by individual Federal Reserve Districts monthly for the period November 1930 to January 1931 and summed. We can pinpoint the Federal Reserve Districts with the highest incidence of suspensions and deposits in suspended banks. Data were revised by the Federal Reserve Board in September 1937, but there are no revised estimates by Federal Reserve District. The largest number of bank closings was concentrated in the St. Louis District with approximately two out of every five suspensions. As we shall see, the closings were related to the failure of the largest regional investment banking house in the South: Caldwell and Company of Nashville, Tennessee. Chicago was second with 15 percent, Richmond 13 percent, Atlanta 11 percent, and Minneapolis 9 percent. These four Districts accounted for one-half of bank suspensions. By including St. Louis these five Districts accounted for 85 percent of the total number of suspensions during the banking crisis. The high concentration in the number of bank suspensions in only five of the twelve Reserve Districts testifies to the region specific character of the crisis.

Deposits in suspended banks tell a different story. Forty-five percent of the deposits of failed banks were in the Federal Reserve Districts of St. Louis and New York. The number of suspensions in New York was negligible (eight), but the closing of the Bank of United States in New York City with $160 million of deposits at the time of suspension explains why New York ranks first. The closing of a single bank in Philadelphia explains most of the deposits in failed banks in that District.

Table 2.2 *Number of bank suspensions, deposits in failed banks monthly during first banking crisis, November 1930–January 1931*

District	No. of banks suspensions				Deposits of failed banks ($m.)			
	Nov. 1930	Dec. 1930	Jan. 1931	Total	Nov. 1930	Dec. 1930	Jan. 1931	Total
Boston	—	5	—	5	—	17	—	17
New York	—	6	2	8	—	188	7	195
Philadelphia	—	6	3	9	—	57	4	61
Cleveland	4	4	7	15	2	1	6	9
Richmond	20	62	18	100	27	34	7	68
Atlanta	16	35	36	87	31	15	24	70
Chicago	14	53	48	115	3	32	17	52
St. Louis	141	97	47	285	133	41	17	191
Minneapolis	27	31	13	71	5	9	4	18
Kansas City	10	16	16	42	5	4	4	13
Dallas	3	8	4	15	2	4	1	7
San Francisco	1	5	3	9	—	6	1	7
Σ*	236	328	197	761	208	408	92	708

Notes: *Totals not the same as given in table 2.1. No revised estimates by Federal Reserve District given in 1937 revision by Federal Reserve.
Source: Board of Governors of the Federal Reserve System, *Federal Reserve Bulletin*, 1976.

The amount of deposits in closed banks in Richmond, Atlanta and Chicago were only 25 percent of the total. There was no panic in either New York City or Philadelphia irrespective of the size of the suspended banks.

Data for individual months show a much higher concentration of suspensions and deposit losses in particular Reserve Districts. The center of the crisis in November was the St. Louis District with 60 percent of bank suspensions and 64 percent of the deposits in failed banks. The Northeast was unaffected by the November crisis; there were no suspensions in the Boston, New York, and Philadelphia Federal Reserve Districts, and only one closing in San Francisco, three in Dallas, and four in Cleveland. Richmond and Atlanta accounted for 15 percent of the suspensions and roughly one-third of the deposits of closed banks. The failure of Caldwell and Company was directly or indirectly responsible for over one-half of the bank closings in the St. Louis, Richmond, and Atlanta Federal Reserve Districts in November. The

November crisis was region specific. There was no nationwide run on the banks nor universal loss of confidence in the US banking system. Moreover, there were no repercussions in the central money markets, in either New York or Chicago.

The center of the crisis in December shifted from St. Louis to New York and Philadelphia if measured solely by deposit losses in closed banks. Deposit losses in these two Districts amounted to 60 percent of the total deposit losses of failed banks. But as we have stated, only two banks – Bank of United States in New York City and Bankers' Trust in Philadelphia – accounted for the lion's share of the losses. Bank suspensions remained moderate in both Districts at six a piece and accelerated in Richmond, Atlanta, and Chicago. Nearly 100 banks failed in the St. Louis District as part of the fallout of the November crisis.

In January 1931 the number of suspensions declined from 328 to 197. However, the decrease in deposits in suspended banks was more dramatic, from $408 million in December to $92 million in January. Two-thirds of the suspensions and deposits were concentrated in three Districts: Chicago, St. Louis, and Atlanta. Bank closings were negligible in Boston, New York, Philadelphia, Dallas, and San Francisco.

Seasonally adjusted data on Federal Reserve Notes in circulation by Federal Reserve Districts are shown in table 2.3 for November and December 1930 and January 1931. The impact of the failure of Caldwell and Company in the St. Louis and Richmond Districts is clear. The unusually large increase in the St. Louis District in November and the increase in the Richmond District in December reveals the strength of the Caldwell collapse. The decline in November of Federal Reserve notes in circulation provides some evidence that increased hoarding was not a problem in eight Districts. Similarly, Boston, Chicago, Kansas City and Dallas show no indications of increased hoarding in December.

The conclusion to which we are inevitably drawn from the diverse data on bank suspensions, deposits in closed banks, and hoarding is that the 1930 banking crisis was region specific; it was not a national crisis, if by that phrase we mean a fairly uniform distribution of bank suspensions and hoarding across the twelve Federal Reserve Districts.

Peter Temin (1990, p. 50) has also expressed some second thoughts about the classification of the accelerated suspensions in November and December 1930 as a national banking panic. In his Lionel Robbins lectures he stated:

I now think that I should have gone further than I did a dozen years ago. The events of late 1930 do not merit the appellation that Friedman and Schwartz bestowed on them.

Table 2.3 *Net change in Federal Reserve notes in circulation seasonally adjusted by Federal Reserve Districts monthly, November 1930–January 1931 ($m.)*

	November	December	January	Change
Boston	−3	−2	+3	−2
New York	+7	+77	0	+84
Philadelphia	−3	+6	−18	−15
Cleveland	−1	+3	+1	+3
Richmond	−1	+18	−1	+16
Atlanta	+1	+5	+8	+14
Chicago	−7	−7	+5	−9
St. Louis	+8	+8	−2	+14
Minneapolis	−2	+2	0	0
Kansas City	−2	0	0	−2
Dallas	−1	0	0	−1
San Francisco	0	+13	+6	+19

Source: Raw data from Board of Governors of the Federal Reserve System, *Federal Reserve Bulletin*. The data were seasonally adjusted by Sandy Hanson using the census X–11 program.

To support his claim that the first banking crisis was a minor event in the history of the Great Depression Temin provided two kinds of evidence. He adjusted the deposits of failed banks in November and December by subtracting the deposits of the two failed banks – Caldwell and Co. and the Bank of United States. The effect was to reduce the magnitude of the bank failures in the 1930 crisis by one-half. He justified the adjustment on the grounds that "Both of the banks had undergone reckless expansion in the late 1920s, and their overblown empires collapsed under the pressure of the emerging Depression" (p. 50), and that there was no rise in short-term interest rates, except in Tennessee. The second bit of evidence he adduced was the behavior of the money stock; there was no change in the money stock of such a magnitude that could have produced such a large macroeconomic effect.

Eugene White (1984) has also cast serious doubts about the causes of the 1930 panic. He questioned the Friedman and Schwartz interpretation that bank failures in 1930 differed from earlier failures in the 1920s; that is, bank illiquidity rather than bank insolvency was the source of the banking disturbances in 1930. White argued that if Friedman and Schwartz were correct the characteristics of bank failures should differ between the two periods. His regression results revealed that during the

November–December panic the balance sheets of failed banks did not differ from failing banks in the 1920s. Although the 1930 suspensions did not differ from earlier years, he did show that bank closings in both 1931 and 1932 did. More will be said about White's study in chapter 5. The cumulative evidence of Temin and White, and also my own, is consistent with the conclusion that the 1930 crisis was a region specific crisis without noticeable national economic effects.

2   The microhistory of the banking crisis

The Federal Reserve has never given an official account of what it thought happened during the 1930 banking crisis. The only reference to the events of the crisis period appeared in the *Federal Reserve Bulletin* in September 1937 (p. 1205) with the publication of revised estimates for bank suspensions and deposits in failed banks 1921–36. On that occasion Reserve officials wrote:

In these months [November–December 1930] 9 large banks in different sections of the country suspended. The closing of these large banks resulted in the closing of many other banks, partly because of affiliate and correspondent relationships, and partly because of the spread of fear among depositors, particularly in territory near the location of the banks.

The nine banks were never identified, but what they thought were the two main characteristics of the crisis emerged: (1) the high correlation of bank suspensions in a few large urban banks and (2) the "local" nature of the effects confined as they were to the "territory near the location of the bank." Both of these insights require further investigation. We examine first the bank failures associated with the collapse of Caldwell and Company in November and second the closing of the Bank of United States in December.

The November failures

The high concentration of bank closings in November in the St. Louis District can be traced to the failure of the investment banking firm of Caldwell and Company of Nashville, Tennessee.[1] The firm controlled

---

[1]   Our knowledge of Caldwell and Company derives from the excellent but neglected study of John McFerrin. The role of Caldwell and Company in generating the November crisis is described by R.W. Goldschmidt (later changed to Goldsmith): *The Changing Structure of American Banking* (London, 1933), p.225. See John Berry McFerrin. *Caldwell and Company* (Nashville, 1969) originally published by the University of North Carolina Press in 1939, and reissued in 1969 by Vanderbilt University Press.

the largest chain of banks in the South with assets in excess of $200 million and also the largest insurance group in the region with assets totalling $230 million. When expanded to include interests in other enterprises, the total equalled at least half a billion dollars. The failure of Caldwell and Company had immediate repercussions in four states, namely Tennessee, Kentucky, Arkansas, and North Carolina in the Atlanta, St. Louis, and Richmond Federal Reserve Districts. Seventy banks failed in Arkansas of which forty-five belonged to the A.B. Banks chain, the stock of which was owned by the Home Insurance Company, a Caldwell affiliate. The fifteen or more banks that closed their doors in Kentucky were either correspondent banks or were directly affiliated with BancoKentucky, a bank holding company that merged with Caldwell in June 1930. Similarly, at least ten bank failures in Tennessee and fifteen in North Carolina can also be traced directly to relationships between Rogers Caldwell and individuals connected with the suspended banks in these states. The collapse of Caldwell and Co.'s financial empire raised expectations of deposit losses in the surrounding region and contributed to bank suspensions in December and January as well.

The beginning of the demise of Caldwell and Co. was heralded on November 7 when the Tennessee Superintendent of Banks recommended that the Bank of Tennessee in Nashville be closed immediately.[2] The bank had deposits of only $10 million and was completely owned and controlled by Caldwell and Co. The Bank of Tennessee was a strange bank. It had no individual deposit customers! Its customers were municipalities and corporations financed by Caldwell. The operations of the bank and Caldwell and Co. were so intertwined that it was difficult to separate the two. Because the bank's closing was announced on Saturday, November 8 and both Sunday and the following Tuesday, November 11 were holidays, it was Wednesday, November 12 before the full repercussions of the failure took effect. On that day two Caldwell affiliates in Knoxville, Tennessee failed to open: The Holston Union National Bank with deposits of $16.5 million and the Holston Trust Co. with deposits of $1.2 million. The runs on these two banks caused runs on all the banks in Knoxville but without further suspensions. On November 14 Caldwell and Company failed and that precipitated a panic in Nashville. Liberty Bank and Trust Co. shut its doors. Although not a Caldwell affiliate, it was dominated by a close friend and associate of Rogers Caldwell.

[2] This description of the collapse of Caldwell and Company is taken mainly from my article: "A Reconsideration of the Causes of the Banking Panic of 1930," *Journal of Economic History*, 40 (September 1980): 571–83.

The panic spread from Nashville to other Caldwell affiliated banks in Memphis, Tennessee without, however, inducing any more suspensions. From the urban centers – Nashville, Knoxville, and Memphis – the fear and uncertainty spread, especially to the correspondent banks of the Holston Union Bank in Knoxville. From the time of the November suspension of the Bank of Tennessee to the end of December nineteen banks failed in the state of Tennessee, sixteen state banks and three national banks most of which were located in eastern Tennessee within the Atlanta Federal Reserve District.

The panic continued to spread. This time to another Caldwell affiliated bank in Little Rock, Arkansas. The bank closed for business on November 15. Correspondent banks were immediately notified and on November 17 forty-three banks failed to open. By November 24, seventy banks in the state had ceased to exist. These were located in agricultural areas that had experienced a rash of bank failures in the twenties. Forty-five of these banks belonged to the A.B. Banks chain, a Caldwell affiliate. The lead bank in the chain was the American Exchange Trust of Little Rock with deposits of $15 million. The alleged withdrawal of over 25 percent of its deposits within a ten day period forced the bank into liquidation. The closing of the remaining forty-five banks in the chain was an inevitable consequence of the chain method of banking organization. Chain banking was a type of multiple office banking in which a number of incorporated banks were controlled by one or more individuals through acquisition of a majority of the stock of newly organized banks. The chain was usually built around and controlled by a key city bank that was much larger than those within the group. The key bank held the reserve balances of the smaller banks, thus increasing their vulnerability to failure when the lead bank encountered difficulties. But banks outside the group failed as well in the wake of the contagion of fear that swept Arkansas. The seventy bank closings in Arkansas represented at least one-half of the bank suspensions in the St. Louis Federal Reserve District in November.

On the same day that the banks closed in Arkansas, panic spread to the Caldwell affiliate in Louisville, Kentucky. BancoKentucky was a bank holding company whose shares had been purchased by two of Louisville's largest banks: The National Bank of Kentucky and the Louisville Trust. BancoKentucky had merged with Caldwell and Company in 1930. The failure of BancoKentucky was directly responsible for the closing of fifteen more Kentucky banks which either were correspondent banks or were directly affiliated with BancoKentucky. The deposits of the two Louisville banks account for one-third of the deposits of failed banks in the St. Louis District in November. Together the Caldwell-related bank suspensions in Arkansas and Kentucky explain 60 percent of the bank suspensions and 70 percent of the deposits in closed banks in the St. Louis District in November.

Contributing to the failures in Arkansas and Kentucky was the agricultural drought in 1930. Hamilton (1985) deserves credit for having resurrected this agricultural catastrophe from historical obscurity and demonstrated its importance in explaining banking suspensions in November and December 1930. The drought extended from the middle Atlantic region to the Ohio and Mississippi river valleys and included large parts of at least fifteen states. The March to August growing season was the driest ever recorded, the fifteen states having had only 57 percent of their natural rainfall. Arkansas was the hardest hit with only 20 percent of its normal rainfall in June and July. Corn yields were off 77 percent in Arkansas, 65 percent in Kentucky, 62 percent in Virginia, and 51 percent in Missouri. The decline in personal income of farm proprietors was more than 50 percent in Arkansas, Mississippi, Maryland, Louisiana, and Oklahoma. The drought simply accelerated the decline in farmers' income already seriously affected by the Great Depression. The repercussions on the banks were serious. Loans to farmers were uncollectible; farm mortgages were in default thereby increasing the amount of frozen assets making the banks more vulnerable to failure. The juxtaposition of the failure of Caldwell and Co. and its bank affiliates together with the prolonged drought captures the principal ingredients of an explanation of the high incidence of bank suspensions in the St. Louis Federal Reserve District. They were both exogenous shocks unrelated to the behavior of current income.

The fourth large bank to fail as a result of the Caldwell collapse was the Central Bank and Trust Co. of Asheville, North Carolina with deposits of $14 million. Central Trust, however, was not an affiliate of the Caldwell group but through a close business associate of Rogers Caldwell the Bank of Tennessee had agreed to a sale of bonds by repurchase agreement to Central Trust and to the purchase of an amount of Revenue Anticipation Notes of the City of Asheville. Depositor knowledge of the relationship between Central Trust and Colonel Luke Lea, an associate of Rogers Caldwell, led to a run on the bank one week after the demise of Caldwell and Co. Fourteen other banks in and around Asheville suspended within three days.

The November panic had at least one of the classic features of a nineteenth-century financial crisis. It had its origins in the failure of a large financial institution that had a complex network of relationships with banks in four surrounding states. Uncertainty and distrust spread instantly to affiliated institutions. The crisis, however, remained regional.

Unlike previous panics, the New York money market was unaffected; that is, no runup of interest rates nor curtailment of credit availability. And, as we have shown, there were no bank suspensions in the Boston, New York, and Philadelphia Federal Reserve Districts. The evidence on the increase of hoarding does not reveal a nationwide response.

McFerrin's (1969) analysis of the failure of Caldwell and Co. and its many affiliates revealed that questionable managerial and financial practices inaugurated in the twenties to foster rapid growth and expansion explain the firm's demise. Poor loans and investments in the twenties contributed to the weakness of the more than 120 banks that closed. McFerrin's interpretation of why the banks failed is consistent with that of White. It is inconsistent with Temin's conjecture that declining prices of lower grade corporate bonds as well as agricultural conditions played a causal role. Agricultural conditions, however, did play a causal role not in the form envisaged by Temin but in the form of an agricultural drought.

The December failures

The failure of two New York City banks and one Philadelphia bank in December account for almost 55 percent of the deposits of failed banks. The Bank of United States (BUS) closed on December 11 with $161 million of total deposits and between 40–45,000 depositors. The Chelsea Bank and Trust closed on December 23 with $19 million of gross deposits. And on December 22 Bankers' Trust of Philadelphia failed to open with deposits of $43 million and 135,000 depositors.

Friedman and Schwartz assign special significance to the Bank of United States' closure. They maintain that the bank's name led to confusion at home and abroad about its official status, thus constituting a more serious blow to depositor confidence than would have been the case had it been any other bank. Bankers allegedly reacted by strengthening their liquidity position, and depositors increased their demands for currency. The evidence they adduced to support their claim was a sharp increase in the currency–deposit ratio in December.

The Bank of United States was incorporated in 1913 with an initial capital of $100,000. By the time its founder Joseph Marcus died in 1908, the bank had $6 million in capital and six branches in New York City. It had a largely ethnic Jewish clientele. His son Bernard Marcus who succeeded him launched a vigorous program of expansion. By a succession of mergers the bank's capital increased to $25 million in 1929, and the number of separate branches increased to fifty-seven. Compared with other New York City banks, its investment in real estate was excessive, and its management practices left much to be desired. The bank closed on December 11, not to be reopened.

The details of the bank's failure are only relevant to the extent that we can show whether its closing contributed to the spread of the banking panic within New York City or the rest of the country; that is, how specifically the number of bank suspensions and deposits in failed banks can be linked directly to the closing of BUS, or what monetary or economic effects it had on the country as a whole.

Two ancillary issues raised by the bank's closing are: Was the bank solvent at the time it failed? and: Why was it that the Federal Reserve Bank of New York and the New York Clearing House Association did not do more to save the bank? These issues are ancillary inasmuch as their significance depends on whether or not the monetary and other economic effects of its demise were important. If they were not, the questions are largely moot.

We begin by asking did the closing of the BUS contribute to the worsening of the panic; that is, can we relate the bank's closing to increased bank suspensions and deposits in failed banks in either New York City or the country as a whole? There was no network of correspondent relationships or affiliated banks either in the Northeast or other parts of the country that were affected directly by its closing. Moreover, as we intend to show later, there were no serious effects on the New York money market. Short-term interest rates remained stable, and at no time was there any signs of credit stringency in the central money market. There was no panic in New York City if by that term we mean the spread of uncertainty indiscriminately engulfing sound and unsound banks alike. The loss of depositor confidence was mainly confined, though not entirely, to BUS customers. If the failure of BUS had diffused uncertainty to the rest of the country, we might have expected losses in failed banks to have been greater in December than in November. However, if we subtract deposit losses in the two New York City banks from total deposit losses in December, we discover that deposit losses in December were only moderately higher than in November – $204 million in November compared with $225 million in December. The highest incidence of bank failures in both November and December were in the same Federal Reserve Districts – St. Louis, Atlanta, and Richmond – which suggests that what was driving the failure rate was the aftershock of the Caldwell suspension rather than the closing of BUS. We may conclude, therefore, from the available evidence that the failure of BUS had negligible effects in contributing to the increased number of bank suspensions in December.

The effects of the November jolt to depositor confidence could reasonably be expected to subside gradually. For example, in mid December twelve Arkansas banks were forced to suspend when the public learned that a director of the closed American Exchange Bank of Little Rock had an interest in eleven of the closed banks. The acceleration of the bank failure rate in the Richmond District in December can be attributed to the fear generated in November with the failure of fourteen Western North Carolina banks. Between December 4 and 20, thirty-three North Carolina banks suspended payment – half of the total failures in the Richmond District in December.

A banking crisis struck the state of Mississippi during the last ten days of December when twenty-five banks closed. Ten banks within a thirty mile radius in the Northeast corner of the state collapsed on December 26. An additional eleven banks failed during the first two weeks of the new year. These sixty-eight bank suspensions in North Carolina and Mississippi can more plausibly be related to the failure of Caldwell and Co. rather than to the failure of BUS.

Friedman and Schwartz's attempt to associate the increase in the currency–deposit ratio in December with the closing of BUS is clouded by the fact that the failure of BUS was not the only conceivable source of the increased demand for currency. We might argue with equal persuasiveness that the resurgence of the failure rate and the amount of hoarding resulted from the secondary effects of the diffusion of fear and uncertainty in the same areas as those affected in November as well as from effects transmitted subsequently to contiguous areas.

3   Interest rates and the banking crisis of 1930

Neither the bank failures of November nor the failure of the BUS in December had serious effects on the New York money market. There certainly was no banking or financial crisis observable in the various money market indicators. The behavior of select short-term interest rates weekly from October through January, 1931 is shown in table 2.4. Following the collapse of the Caldwell banking network in the two weeks after November 8, the prime commercial paper rate *fell* from 3 percent to 2.88 percent where it remained through the end of December. The rate on ninety-day prime bankers' acceptances remained unchanged during the entire three-month period. The new call money rate did not change during November and increased only thirty basis points in the two weeks following the closing of BUS on December 11.

Rates charged on commercial loans by nineteen reporting banks are shown in table 2.5. The reporting banks are classified: New York City, seven Northern and Eastern cities, and eleven Southern and Western

Table 2.4 *Short-term interest rates in New York City weekly, October 1930–January 1931*

Month	Prime commercial paper 4–6 months	Prime bankers' acceptance 90 days	Average rate new call loans stock market
October			
4	3.00	1.88	1.90
11	3.00	1.88	2.00
18	3.00	1.88	2.00
25	3.00	1.88	2.00
November			
1	3.00	1.88	2.00
8	3.00	1.88	2.00
15	2.88	1.88	2.00
22	2.88	1.88	2.00
29	2.88	1.88	2.00
December			
6	2.88	1.88	2.00
13	2.88	1.88	2.09
20	2.88	1.88	2.21
27	2.88	1.88	2.04
January			
3	2.88	1.88	2.94
10	2.88	1.75	1.50
17	2.88	1.63	1.50
24	2.88	1.50	1.50
31	2.75	1.44	1.50

Source: Board of Governors of the Federal Reserve System, *Banking and Monetary Statistics: 1914–1941*, Washington DC, 1976, pp. 456–7.

Table 2.5 *Rates charged on commercial loans by banks in principal cities, October 1930–January 1931*

Month	New York City	7 North and Eastern cities	11 South and Western cities
October	3.92	4.49	5.18
November	3.79	4.38	5.17
December	3.82	4.38	5.01
January	3.74	4.23	5.01

Source: Board of Governors of Federal Reserve System, *Banking and Monetary Statistics, 1914–1941*, Washington DC, 1976, p. 464.

Table 2.6 *US government and corporate bond yields monthly, October 1930–January 1931*

Month	US Bonds	Corporate Aaa	Corporate Baa
October	3.21	4.42	5.94
November	3.19	4.47	6.25
December	3.22	4.52	6.71
January	3.20	4.42	6.41

Source: Board of Governors of Federal Reserve System, *Banking and Monetary Statistics, 1914–1941*, Washington, DC, November 1943, p. 470.

cities. The failure of the Caldwell banks had no tightening effects on the commercial loan rate in any of the cities. In fact, the rate fell in all three classifications in November. Neither is there a discernible effect on the loan rate in December. The rate in New York City increased a minuscule 3 basis points and either remained unchanged or fell in the other eighteen cities.

There is no evidence from short-term interest rate data of any kind of crisis in the New York money market in either November or December. The collapse of the BUS is not discernible in any of the money market indicators. The absence of any effects on short-term interest rates distinguishes what happened in the final months of 1930 from all of the pre-1914 banking crises.

Longer-term interest rates are shown in table 2.6. Yields on long-term US government securities remain virtually unchanged. Corporate bonds rated Aaa increased ten basis points between October and December. The most perceptible effects were observable in the corporate Baa market with yields increasing seventy-seven basis points most of which occurred in December. Nevertheless, the bond markets remained calm and orderly with no evidence of a crisis of confidence. Friedman and Schwartz (1963, p. 312) attributed the widening gap between long-term safe government securities and riskier corporate bonds to the banks' increased demand for liquidity. Although they did not say the deteriorating prices of lower-grade securities contributed to the 1930 crisis, they did state emphatically that it was a factor in subsequent banking crises.

Another relevant rate for measuring monetary stringency during a banking panic is the short-term rate on bank loans in local markets. We have seen that rates in New York City in November were not sensitive to the regional banking crisis generated by the failure of Caldwell and Company. Nor were rates sensitive to the failure of BUS. Customer loan rates are available for leading cities in the monthly *Federal Reserve Bulletin*. Prior to March 1939 each bank reported a prevailing rate or range of rates charged to customers on the bulk of commercial loans as of the week ending on the 15th of each month. Rates were also reported monthly for four outstanding kinds of loans: prime commercial paper, loans secured by prime stock exchange collateral, loans secured by warehouse receipts, and interbank loans. Table 2.7 shows the behavior of interest rates for the months of October–December 1930.

What is readily apparent from table 2.7 is the absence of "liquidity" or portfolio balance effects produced by the destruction of deposits in those cities most affected by the banking crisis. The failure of the largest bank in Arkansas in November, for example, produced no change in customer loan rates in Little Rock except to widen the range on interbank loans from 6 to 6.7 percent. The effects on loan rates in other cities, Nashville, Louisville, and Charlotte, North Carolina were likewise negligible. There is certainly nothing in this evidence on local loan rates to suggest a monetary disturbance of major or even minor importance. If regional credit markets are interlocked with the national market, then it is understandable why we do not observe any perceptible changes in customer loan rates in New York City.

The behavior of customer loan rates however may not be a reliable indicator of the effects of local banking crises. The availability of credit is not reflected in the loan rate data. If small business financing is bank specific, then bank suspensions may decrease the supply of loanable funds and thereby jeopardize firm solvency. Moreover, the effects of a local banking crisis, though not observable in customer loan rates may, nevertheless, exert an appreciable effect on local and regional expenditures. Conceivably households as well as business firms might respond to a total loss of check-using transactions balances by reducing deposit-using expenditures. The decline in expenditures should be reflected in a marked decrease in bank debits, especially in those areas where the incidence of bank suspensions was the highest. The decline in bank debits will almost certainly exaggerate the extent and size of the expenditure reduction since households may attempt to substitute currency-using for some check-using expenditures. But it would be a very strong assumption, indeed, to assert that the decline in bank debits was offset completely by an increase in the velocity of currency.

Table 2.7 *Behavior of loan rates in five cities where the incidence of bank failures was the highest, October–December 1930*

	Prime commercial paper	Loans secured by stock exchange collateral	Loans secured by warehouse receipts	Interbank loans
Nashville, Tennessee				
October	6	6	5.5–6	5.5–6
November	6	6	5.5–6	5.5–6
December	6–8	6–8	6–8	6
Louisville, Kentucky				
October	6	5.5–6	6	5–5.5
November	6	5.5–6	6	5–5.5
December	6	5.5–6	6	5
Little Rock, Arkansas				
October	6	6–7	6–7	6
November	6	6–7	6–7	6–7
December	6	6	6–6.5	6
Charlotte, North Carolina[a]				
October	5–6	5.75–6	6	6
November	5–6	5.5–6	5.5–6	6
December	5–6	5.5–6	5.5–6	6
New York City, NY[b]				
October	3.75–4	4–5	4–5	4–4.5
November	3.5–4	4–5	4–5	4–4.5
December	3.5–4	4–5	4–5	4–4.5

Notes: [a] Asheville, North Carolina was not included as a reporting city. Charlotte, North Carolina has been substituted.
[b] Although there was only one bank failure in New York City, the loss of deposits was greater than all of the other cities combined.
Source: Board of Governors of the Federal Reserve System, *Federal Reserve Bulletin*, January 1931, p. 23.

4   Expenditure effects of the banking crisis

In a previous study Wicker (1982) used bank debit data to explore the expenditure effects attributable to panic-induced bank suspensions.[3] There are two separate sources of estimates for both monthly bank debit

---

[3]   Much of the material in this section is contained in my article: "Interest Rate and Expenditure Effects of the Banking Panic of 1930," *Explorations in Economic History*, 19 (July, 1982): 435–45.

behavior for the period 1919–32. The *Standard Statistical Base Book Bulletin* includes monthly bank debit data for 201 cities and pooled by state seasonally adjusted and unadjusted. The Federal Reserve Board also compiled estimates of seasonally adjusted bank debits monthly for 141 cities and pooled by Federal Reserve District.

The evidence is strong that there is a close relationship between bank debits and expenditures for final output (GNP), especially for bank debits outside New York City where the volume of purely financial transactions is not very large. Between 1929 and 1933, for example, GNP declined 47 percent whereas bank debits outside New York City decreased 57 percent. Schwartz (1981) employed monthly bank debits as a proxy for income in performing Granger–Sims causality tests for the period 1919–39. She found that there is a very high correlation between monthly personal income and monthly bank debits outside New York City for the period 1929–33 without lags and with or without removal of long-term trends. There are no data, however, on the behavior of bank debits and income generating expenditures either by city or by state during the Great Depression.

To discern the impact of the first banking crisis in table 2.8 we classify Federal Reserve Districts according to number of bank suspensions in November and December 1930 and for select years. We compare the percentage change in seasonally adjusted bank debits between October and December 1930 with the corresponding interval of the stock market crash (1929) and a less disturbed year 1928. Three inferences may be drawn from the evidence presented in table 2.8. First, bank debits declined uniformly two to three times more rapidly during the stock market crash than during the 1930 banking panic. Second, bank debits declined in 1930 by as much in Federal Reserve Districts with eleven or fewer failures as they did in Districts with eighty or more suspensions; the notable exception was the St. Louis Federal Reserve District, the focal point of the banking crisis in November. Third, the severity of the decline in the final quarters of 1929 and 1930 is readily apparent from the behavior of bank debits in the less-disturbed year 1928.

Although the impact of the banking panic of 1930 is clearly discernible in the behavior of bank debits in the St. Louis District, the absolute magnitude of the disturbance is obscured by comparison with percentage rates of change. In addition, it is the absolute size of the change in debits as a proxy for expenditures that discloses the overall impact or what the overall impact on the economy may have been. In November 1930 the proportion of debits in the St. Louis District to total bank debits outside New York City was 4.7 percent, or somewhat less than $1 billion out of a total of approximately $20 billion. The 15 percent decrease in the

Table 2.8 *Percentage change in seasonally adjusted bank debits by Federal Reserve District classified by number of bank suspensions in November–December 1930 for the final quarters of 1928, 1929, and 1930*

	No. of failures Nov.–Dec.	Change in bank debits seasonally adjusted Oct.–Dec. (%)		
Federal Reserve District	1930	1928	1929	1930
I Eleven failures or less				
1. New York	6	8.5	−41.0^a	−11.9
2. Philadelphia	6	4.8	−11.5	−1.3
3. Cleveland	8	−2.9	−19.9	−5.8
4. Dallas	11	1.5	−14.2	−7.1
5. San Francisco	6	2.9	b	b
6. Boston	5	6.0	−24.1	−12.0
II More than eleven, less than eighty				
7. Kansas City	26	6.0	−9.8	−4.5
8. Atlanta	51	4.8	−12.0	−6.9
9. Minneapolis	58	−12.3	−6.5	2.5
10. Chicago	67	8.3	−23.8	−4.7
III More than eighty				
11. Richmond	82	b	−13.1	−4.9
12. St. Louis	238	4.2	−16.7	−14.8

Notes: ^{a} Inflated by the large amount of purely financial transactions in New York City.
^{b} Less than 1 percent.
Source: US Department of Commerce, *Survey of Current Business*, Washington DC, January 1931, no. 113, p. 21.

St. Louis debits between October and December 1930 amounted to a decrease of probably not much more than $150 million, less than a 1 percent change in total debits outside New York City. The inference is clearly warranted that there were identifiable expenditure effects of the banking crisis in November and December in the St. Louis District. But the magnitude of the effect in relation to the behavior of total bank debits was not very great.

The behavior of bank debits during the banking crisis of 1930 and the stock market debacle of 1929 conforms closely to the performance of the industrial production index. The index declined 15.3 percent between October and December 1929 and 5.7 percent during the comparable period in 1930. The difference is not as marked as in the behavior of department store sales, factory employment, and payrolls. The evidence

Table 2.9 *Percentage decline in bank debits seasonally adjusted October–December for select years by city where 1930 panic-induced suspensions were the highest*

City	Average 1922–28	Percentage change in bank debits				
		1929	1930	1931	1932	1933
Little Rock	−7.3	−18.0	−41.7	2.9	5.1	14.1
Louisville	0.0	−28.0	−30.9	−7.9	−4.0	2.1
Nashville	−13.6	−6.8	−15.7	0.0	5.5	7.2
Memphis	−5.6	−31.0	−23.7	−13.6	−26.7	−24.1
Asheville	−7.0	−2.0	−48.9	−11.9	−7.5	−6.0

Source: Standard Statistical Base Book Bulletin, Standard Trade and Security Services, Statistical Section, March 1932 and April 1934.

from the bank debit data clearly reveals that the direct and immediate expenditure effects of the stock market crash were substantially greater than they had been during the banking crisis of 1930.

We can now examine in richer detail expenditure effects of bank suspensions in those cities and states that were in the eye of the financial hurricane. Table 2.9 shows the percentage decline in bank debits during the final quarter of select years in the five cities where the incidence of the panic was the highest. The severity of the crisis is particularly apparent in the cities of Little Rock and Asheville where seasonally adjusted bank debits declined by more than 40 percent, a dramatic decline in check-using transactions.

Although the decline in debits in Louisville and Memphis was substantial in 1930 relative to the pre-1929 and post-1930 years, their behavior was similar in both 1929 and 1930. We are, therefore, unable to identify any special expenditure effects resulting solely from bank suspensions. Debits declined least during the banking crisis in Nashville, Tennessee but substantially more than in 1929. The dramatic reduction in the percentage rate of decline in bank debits in the final quarters of 1931 and 1933 reveals again how serious the banking disturbances in 1930 really were. Together these five cities absorbed the urban impact of the banking panic. Even if we allow generously for the substitution of currency-using for check-using transactions, the effect on final payments of the decline in debits must have been substantial in the five cities most affected by the panic.

Can we estimate quantitatively the absolute magnitude of the decline in check-using expenditures as reflected in the behavior of bank debits in the four cities most affected? Standard Statistical Service data provide no benchmark estimates for any month or year of the dollar amount of debits for either individual cities or states. The Federal Reserve Board, however, computed indices of the annual average of monthly bank debits by city and Federal Reserve District using 1919 as the base year. The Board also provided estimates of average monthly debits, seasonally adjusted in millions of dollars for the base year for select cities within each of the twelve Federal Reserve Districts.

Table 2.10 shows average monthly estimates of the dollar amount of bank debits for four of the five cities where the panic was centered. Bank debits declined by approximately $100 million between 1929 and 1930 in these four cities. The data do not, of course, reveal anything about the size of the decline in debits attributable to the panic in November–December 1930. Annual monthly averages obscure the sharp decline in bank debits in the final quarter of the year. Nevertheless, the data do enable us to form a clearer idea of the relative magnitudes of the panic-induced expenditure declines by city, even after making liberal allowance for the understatement of the behavior of bank debits in annual averages of monthly data.

5   The banking crisis as a cause of the Great Depression

The banking crisis of 1930 has special significance among the four banking crises of the Great Depression because of the causal role assigned to it by Friedman and Schwartz. They maintained that an autonomous disturbance in the currency–deposit ratio provoked a rash of bank suspensions that decreased the money stock which, in turn, converted a mild downturn into a major depression. They conjectured that "In October [sic] 1930, the monetary character of the contraction changed dramatically. ... A contagion of fear spread among depositors, starting from agricultural areas, which had experienced the heaviest impact of bank failures in the twenties" (p. 308). Poor loans and investments in the 1920s was not in their judgment the principal factor contributing to the accelerated rate of bank suspensions. They did not attempt to analyze or to identify empirically the determinants of the currency–deposit ratio. They simply assumed that interest rates and income were not statistically significant determinants of that ratio.

To have exerted a causal role, panic-induced bank suspensions must have been exogenous; that is, independent of prior changes in interest rates and income. On the other hand, Peter Temin (1976) has maintained

Table 2.10 *Annual monthly averages of dollar amounts of bank debits for cities where the incidence of banking panic was the highest*

City	Monthly average ($ million) 1919	Annual monthly averages ($ million)		Percentage change 1929–30
		1929	1930	
Little Rock	36	75.1	57.3	−24.0
Louisville	156	210.3	182.1	−13.4
Nashville	93	110.5	90.6	−18.0
Memphis	136	183.1	142.0	−22.4
Totals	421	579.0	472.0	−18.5
St. Louis Federal Reserve District (5 centers)	965	1,326.9	1,103.0	−16.9
US (141 centers)	37,446	77,963.0	55,195.0	−29.2

Source: US Department of Commerce, *Survey of Current Business*, Washington, DC, January 1931, no. 113, p. 21.

that the 1930 banking failures were endogenous; they depended mainly on agricultural conditions prevalent in the high failure rate areas. To discriminate between Friedman and Schwartz's two conceivable causes of bank suspensions – a higher failure rate in areas of agricultural distress and in areas with the most suspensions in the 1920s – Temin concluded that bank closings in 1930 were not the result of poor loans and investments made in the twenties but were caused by changes in agricultural conditions, although he admitted the link was by no means clear. Temin failed to recognize that an agricultural drought might have exercised a depressing effect on agricultural prices and incomes quite apart from the effects of the decline in economic activity. Nevertheless, he acknowledged that the search for the causes of bank failures by regression studies might be unsatisfactory and conjectured that the decline in the prices of lower-grade corporate bonds was an important influence that operated equally on all banks before the November panic. However, Temin produced no evidence to support his conjecture. Without data on the portfolios of suspended banks, he could not show how the decline in bond prices had contributed to the specific failures in November and December.

White's (1984, p. 127) econometric study of bank failures during the 1930 panic also showed that bond holdings of national banks were not a source of trouble. Solvency did not appear to be affected by their bond holdings. Although he did not find econometric support for Temin's hypothesis, he claimed that the limited evidence for state banks (Vermont and Michigan) did.

The evidence from bank failures in Arkansas limited though it might be does not support Temin's claim. Garlock and Gile (1935) concluded from a sample of closed banks that depreciation of security prices was not a major cause of bank failures in Arkansas between 1930 and 1932. The volume of securities carried into the Depression by the closed banks was not sufficient to have caused their failure. More than 65 percent of the suspended banks closed their doors before the bond market had become severely depressed (p. 35). The evidence about the causes of the bank failures in Arkansas in 1930 is inconsistent with Temin's regression results that poor loans and investments in the twenties do not explain the bank failure rate in 1930 and with his conjecture that the decline in the prices of lower-grade corporate bonds was an important influence operating on bank solvency. The bank suspensions in Arkansas were not insignificant. They accounted for at least one-third of total bank suspensions in November and more than one-half after the onset of the panic in the middle of the month.

Neither Friedman and Schwartz nor Temin attempted to provide econometric evidence to support their conflicting claims about the exogeneity or endogeneity of bank failures. Anderson and Butkiewicz (1980) attempted to remedy this alleged gap in our knowledge by constructing a structural model where both income and the bank failure rate are endogenous variables. They found that the money supply function was not influenced by either interest rates or income but was significantly affected by bank failures. Seventy-two percent of the decline in the money stock could be attributed to the bank failure variable. They could not reject the hypothesis that bank failures were an important cause of the decline in the money stock during the Great Depression.

Boughton and Wicker (1979 and 1984) agreed with Anderson and Butkiewicz that bank failures were an important part of the explanation for the behavior of the money stock between 1930 and 1933. But, contrary to Anderson and Butkiewicz, they demonstrated that interest rates and income were also important determinants of the money stock. The effect on the money stock worked through the currency–deposit ratio. Boughton and Wicker estimated the currency–deposit ratio for the period November 1930 to March 1933 and found that bank failures accounted for 28.3 percent of the explained portion of the ratio, declining interest rates accounted for another 32.6 percent, and falling expenditures 12.8 percent. The finding that the currency–deposit ratio was interest sensitive was consistent with Temin's view that causation went from income and interest rates to money. Paul Trescott (1984) reestimated the Boughton–Wicker regression equations using their data. He found that bank failures were the chief cause of the currency outflows, and that interest rates did not have significant influence. The best explanation for this seeming anomaly between Trescott's and Boughton and Wicker's findings may be that a large number of bank failures prior to March 1933, with the single exception for 1930, were the result, not the cause, of the rise in the currency–deposit ratio. Trescott's regressions may increase the degree of feedback, raising the measured correlation but biasing upward the estimated effects of bank failures. Trescott also assembled evidence from contemporary sources showing that the bulk of the bank failures in 1930, and an appreciable number in 1931, can be viewed as exogenous in relation to the decline in income.

To assess what happened to the money stock during the banking crisis, we employ Friedman and Schwartz's seasonally adjusted M-1 and M-2. M-1 refers to currency held by the public plus demand deposits, and M-2 includes M-1 plus time deposits. Table 2.11 shows the monthly changes in each of these monetary aggregates from the beginning of the Great Depression in August 1929 to April 1931.

Between November and January 1931 M-1 declined by $425 million and M-2 by $1,400 million. But the $425 million decline in M-1 when compared with similar declines earlier in 1930 was not especially large. For example, between January and March 1930 M-1 declined by $620 million; between April and June 1930 by $1 billion, and between August and October $414 million. Why, we might ask, attribute serious output effects solely to the banking crisis quarter when the changes in M-1 were either of the same magnitude or greater in earlier quarterly episodes? Moreover, the decrease in M-1 during the two most serious crisis months was only $64 million; it rose in November by $41 million and fell by $105 million in December. It remains a puzzle why the 608 bank suspensions with $552 million of deposit losses in November and December failed to have a greater effect on M-1.

The Friedman and Schwartz inference about the serious output effects of the first banking crisis derives solely from the behavior of M-2. Total deposits declined by $1.2 billion, $900 million of which was time deposits and only $279 million demand deposits. We may raise the same question about the behavior of M-2 that we raised about M-1. M-2 had declined by $950 million in the second quarter of 1930. Why did Friedman and Schwartz fail to attribute output effects to the decrease earlier in 1930?

The determinants of the money stock are shown in table 2.12. The three main determinants are: monetary base, the currency–deposit ratio, and the demand deposit–time deposits ratio. The monetary base and the currency–deposit ratio increased in every month of the banking crisis.

Table 2.11 *Changes in M-1 and M-2 seasonally adjusted, August 1929–March 1931 ($m.)*

	1929		1930		1931	
	M1	M2	M1	M2	M1	M2
January			−757	−572	−361	−401
February			−261	+163	+152	+289
March			+398	+695	+45	−110
April			−401	−513	−508	−422
May			−610	−467		
June			−32	+30		
July			+107	+40		
August	−212	−122	−339	−249		
September	−56	−41	−19	−14		
October	+2,000	+1,918	−56	−26		
November	−2,761	−3,117	+41	−314		
December	+931	+839	−105	−686		

Source: Milton Friedman and Anna Schwartz, *A Monetary History of the United States*, Princeton, 1963, pp. 712–13.

Table 2.12 *Determinants of the money stock, October 1930–January 1931*

	Monetary base ($b.)	Currency/deposit	Time deposit/ demand deposit
1930			
October	6.8	0.087	0.939
November	6.9	0.090	0.923
December	7.1	0.095	0.905
1931			
January	7.2	0.099	0.921

Source: Milton Friedman and Anna Schwartz, *A Monetary History of the United States*, Princeton, 1963, pp. 803 and 713.

There was a significant reduction in the demand deposit–time deposit ratio in December. The public was shifting out of time deposits at a faster rate than demand deposits, the effect of which was, other things being equal, expansionary, not contractionary. Both the increase in the monetary base and the decline in the time deposit–demand deposit ratios were expansionary. The entire effect of the decline in M-2 in November and December is attributable to the increase in the currency–deposit ratio.

Friedman and Schwartz were not alone in assigning a causal role to bank suspensions in causing output to change during the Great Depression. Ben Bernanke (1983) also regarded widespread bank failures as causally significant. However, unlike Friedman and Schwartz, who emphasized the relationship between money and output, he looked to the supply of bank credit as the nonmonetary channel through which financial distress exerted real effects. Bank failures increased the real cost of financial intermediation (information gathering and nontrivial market making) thereby making credit more expensive and more difficult to obtain. He also argued that the increase in the cost of intermediation affected small companies and consumers far more than large firms. By adding credit proxies to a Barro-like (1977) regression, he showed that they improved the purely monetary explanation of short-run movements in output. Nevertheless, historical evidence is still lacking about any direct relationship between bank credit and output. Although Bernanke agreed that the decrease in the money stock was important, he doubted whether it provided a complete explanation for the decline in output during the Great Depression. And he does not address the issue of the behavior of bank credit and output specifically during the 1930 banking crisis.

Temin (1990) devised a test of Bernanke's hypothesis that smaller firms would be affected more than larger firms by the increased cost of intermediation. He simulated cross-sectional regressions to determine the effects of a fall in production in various sized industries for three time periods. The first two look at the decline immediately after the crisis up until Britain left gold in September 1931. He found that all of the coefficients of the Bernanke regressions have the wrong sign; that is, in the more concentrated industries, the largest fifty firms suffered the largest decline in production.

The evidence on the causal role of money and bank credit aggregates in explaining the Great Depression remains in many important respects highly ambivalent. The collapse of Caldwell and Company and the Bank of United States appear to be unrelated to events brought on by the Great Depression. Managerial ineptness encompassing both poor loans and investments in the twenties and questionable legal practices deserve a fair share of the blame for the demise of both Caldwell and Company and the Bank of United States. Furthermore, the devastating agricultural drought in the South during the summer of 1930 played an important ancillary role in accounting for the high incidence of bank suspensions in primarily agricultural regions. The historical evidence on which this inference is based is largely consistent with the Friedman and Schwartz view of the 1930 banking crisis as a purely autonomous disturbance unrelated to prior movements in income and interest rates.

Some of the econometric evidence is also consistent with the Friedman and Schwartz view. Anderson and Butkiewicz, for example, could not reject the hypothesis that bank failures were an important cause of the decline in the money stock. Trescott also found that bank failures were the chief cause of currency outflows and ultimately of the money stock.

All of the econometric evidence, however, does not point in the same direction. Although Boughton and Wicker found that bank failures were a significant determinant of the money stock between 1930 and 1933, they demonstrated that interest rates and income were important determinants of the money stock through the currency–deposit ratio. And White was able to show that bank suspensions in 1930 did not differ from the experience of the 1920s. Moreover, the evidence from bank debit data does not support the view that the expenditure effects of the 1930 crises were large. The resolution of this debate requires a reconciliation of the historical and econometric evidence.

6   The role of the Federal Reserve in the banking crisis

We are now prepared to ask as well as attempt to answer the question: What was the Federal Reserve's response to the acceleration of bank suspensions and increased hoarding in November and December 1930? Fed behavior can be discerned from three items on the balance sheets of each of the twelve Federal Reserve Banks; bills discounted, bills bought, and government security holdings. We have every reason to have expected a positive response since the Fed was established allegedly to prevent banking crises in the central money market. That task Fed officials performed successfully in November and December 1930. The money market remained calm and stable even after the failure of BUS. Domestic hoarding subsided in January. Nevertheless, there was no return flow of currency to the banking system, except for the normal seasonal inflow. The loss of depositor confidence was reflected in the increased demand for currency relative to deposits. We will discuss the Fed's response in two stages: the first describes what the Fed did following the failure of Caldwell and Company in November, and the second describes Fed action in the wake of the closing of BUS.

Stage 1 Failure of Caldwell and Company

Although Caldwell's Bank of Tennessee closed on Saturday, November 8, Sunday and the following Tuesday were bank holidays. It was

Table 2.13 *Leading determinants of member bank reserves,* November 12–December 10, 1930*

	November 12	December 10	±
Bills discounted	192	257	+65
Bills bought	207	244	+37
Government securities	601	617	+16
Currency in circulation	4,190	4,369	+179
Gold stock	4,262	4,289	+27
Reserves	2,490	2,448	−42

Note: * Wednesday figures.
Source: Board of Governors of the Federal Reserve System, *Banking and Monetary Statistics*, Washington DC, 1976, p. 385.

Wednesday, November 12 before the full repercussions began to take effect. The behavior of member bank reserves between November 12 and December 10 is shown in table 2.13. It reveals the extent of Fed involvement during the first stage of the banking crisis prior to the closing of BUS.

There was an increase of $179 million in currency in circulation, in both seasonal and nonseasonal demands, between the time Caldwell failed and the closure of BUS. The increase was offset to the extent of $160 million by increases in bills discounted, bills bought, government security purchases and increases in the gold stock. More than one-half of the increase in currency was offset by increases in bills bought (57 percent); 10 percent by purchases of government securities and nearly 25 percent by increases in the gold stock. The lion's share of the adjustment fell on bills discounted and bills bought with a relatively minor role for government security purchases.

Aggregate reserve behavior conceals the response of the individual Federal Reserve Banks to the banking disturbances in the individual Districts. One might have expected a positive response in those areas where the incidence of bank suspensions was especially high. The responsibility for administering the discount window rested with the officials of the individual Reserve Banks. Moreover, each Bank had some discretion to acquire or dispose of government securities outside the Open Market Investment Account, the responsibility for which rested with the Open Market Policy Conference.

As we have previously shown, the incidence of bank failures and hoarding was greatest in the three Reserve Districts of St. Louis, Richmond, and Atlanta. With the exception of the St. Louis Fed the

WITHDRAWN
SCCCC - LIBRARY
4601 Mid Rivers Mall Drive
St. Peters, MO 63376

Table 2.14 *Changes in credit extended by the twelve Federal Reserve Banks between November 12 and December 3, 1930*

Federal Reserve District	Bills discounted	Bills bought	Government securities	Total
Richmond	0.2	0.8	8.5	9.5
St. Louis	−2.4	0.3	−9.7	−11.8
Atlanta	2.8	0.2	5.1	8.1
New York	14.2	4.5	−44.9	−26.2
Philadelphia	2.6	0.4	1.2	4.2
Boston	3.2	2.2	1.1	6.5
Cleveland	9.0	−0.7	1.4	9.7
Chicago	6.2	2.4	2.3	10.9
Minneapolis	0.2	1.0	0.5	1.7
Kansas City	2.2	1.1	0.9	1.2
Dallas	−1.0	−0.5	0.8	0.2
San Francisco	7.8	3.6	1.5	12.9

Source: Commercial and Financial Chronicle, November–December 1930.

response of the other two Federal Reserve Banks was exactly as anticipated. Presumably, a regional banking crisis should have evoked increased support to member banks in the form of an infusion of Federal Reserve Credit. However, this did not happen at the St. Louis Fed where the incidence of bank suspensions was the highest following the failure of Caldwell and Company. The response of each Federal Reserve Bank is shown in table 2.14. Federal Reserve Credit declined at the St. Louis Fed by $12 million between November 12 and December 3; it also declined by $26 million in New York where the sale of securities more than offset the increase in bills discounted and bills bought. Bills discounted declined by $2.4 million at the St. Louis Fed. In no other District was there a decrease, except Dallas. Government security holdings declined by $10 million as well. The failure of the St. Louis Bank to respond to the banking crisis by increasing accommodation may be explained if bank suspensions were largely confined to nonmember banks and if member banks were not subjected to enough pressure to require Federal Reserve support. Of course, it is conceivable that the St. Louis Fed deliberately made borrowing more difficult, but there is no evidence whatsoever to support such a claim.

The response of the Richmond and Atlanta Federal Reserve Banks was consistent with what we might have anticipated. Bills discounted, bills bought, and government securities purchased increased more in these two Districts than all other Districts with the single exception of the Cleveland District.

During the four weeks following the failure of Caldwell and Company the New York Fed's response was contractionary. Although bills discounted and bills bought increased by almost $20 million, security holdings decreased by $45 million. The response of the New York Bank reveals that there was no crisis in the New York money market, not that their behavior was perverse.

Stage 2 Failure of Bank of United States

The second stage of the banking crisis began with the collapse of the Bank of United States in New York City on December 11. In the weeks immediately following the collapse of BUS, officials of the Federal Reserve Bank of New York with the support of the Clearing House banks proposed a plan whereby BUS would merge with three other New York City banks: Manufacturers Trust, Public National, and International Trust Company. The merger, if it had been successful, would have created the fourth largest bank in the City and would have infused some $30 million of new capital to be provided by the Clearing House banks. Reserve officials of the New York Bank were attentive to the consequences if BUS were allowed to fail. Nevertheless, at the last moment negotiations broke down. The Clearing House banks rejected the terms of the proposed merger agreement.

Controversy still surrounds attempts to explain why the merger was not consummated. Friedman (1974, p. 201) assigned a role to anti-Semitism as a contributing factor to the merger breakdown. He stated:

Anti-Semitism almost surely played a role in the decision of the Clearing House to reject the New York Bank's plan. For most members of the Clearing House, the evidence to this effect is indirect. It is much less so for those dominated by J.P. Morgan and Co. We know how John Piermont Morgan, Jr. the head of the house of Morgan felt about Jews, thanks to an entry in the diary of Charles Hamlin.

The evidence to which Friedman refers is gossip, reliable gossip perhaps for all we know, but an awfully thin reed on which to hang the merger collapse.

Lucia (1985, p. 409) claims that there were at least five better reasons why the Clearing House bankers rejected the merger: (1) fear of potential portfolio losses at BUS; (2) fear of possible lawsuits by stockholders of BUS and other participating banks; (3) the existence of past agreements to repurchase BUS stock at a fixed price; (4) difficulty of obtaining agreement among stockholders within a reasonable time frame because of wide dispersion of ownership of BUS stock, and (5) a deep distrust of officers and management of BUS.

But irrespective of why the Clearing House banks withdrew their support, the question remains why the Federal Reserve Bank of New York did not on its own initiative do more to prevent BUS from closing. The New York Superintendent of Banking – Joseph A. Broderick – later testified that the BUS was solvent at the time it failed implying more might have been done by the New York Fed. If, on the other hand, the bank was insolvent the case for saving it would be considerably weakened. The weight of the evidence as it appears in the archives of the Federal Reserve Bank of New York seems to suggest that the BUS was insolvent in December 1930. Lucia (1985), Friedman and Schwartz (1986), Trescott (1992), and O'Brien (1992) now appear to agree that the bank was insolvent; its assets were not equal to its liabilities, though the shortfall was not large. There is nothing in central bank lore relating to banking panics that obligated the central bank to provide support for an insolvent bank. Solvency or insolvency as Friedman and Schwartz (1986, p. 199) have stated was not the key issue. The key issue was what effects the closing of the BUS might have on monetary and economic developments in the country as a whole. Although the matter still remains in dispute, it is far from clear from all the evidence available that the closing of BUS was instrumental in exacerbating the panic in December. Bank closings and deposit losses in December can equally well, if not better, be explained by the reverberations of the collapse of Caldwell and Company in November including the effects on the currency–deposit ratio.

Once the bank was allowed to fail, however, the chief task of the New York Fed was to contain the effects of the bank's closing and to prevent any further disturbance to the New York money market. In the face of large depositor withdrawals, the New York Fed purchased for its own account $40 million of government securities on Saturday, December 13. Federal Reserve notes in circulation in the New York District increased $71 million between December 11 and December 17 and another $46 million in the following statement week. Bills discounted and bills bought increased $103 million. Increased accommodation at the discount window and the purchase of acceptances plus security purchases were able to more than offset the effects of increased hoarding on bank reserves. Nevertheless, reserves fell by $57 million. The increase in Federal Reserve notes in circulation relative to the fall in reserve deposits led to an increase in the monetary base.

Purchases for the open market account totalled $33 million on December 30 and 31, but an additional $10 million were acquired outside the regular open market account. The Committee disposed of the securities during the first and second weeks of January and did not engage in any further operations before May. The action of the New York Fed insured stability in the New York money market without resorting to the suspension of cash payments or the issue of Clearing House Certificates as in pre-1914 financial crises.

7   What should the Fed have done?

We have attempted to describe what the Fed did during the November–January banking crisis. It was successful in maintaining stability in the central money market; there was no banking panic in New York City for which Federal Reserve officials deserve full credit. The New York Fed displayed leadership and initiative in attempting to obtain a merger agreement which, if successful, would have saved BUS.

The actions of the Federal Reserve, however, did not restore depositor confidence although bank suspensions, deposits in failed banks and hoarding decelerated rapidly in January 1931. There was no dishoarding. At the January 21, 1931 meeting of the Open Market Policy Conference it was reported that the currency requirement in addition to the normal seasonal demand between the middle of November and the first of January had been about $300 million:

Since the first of the year the return of currency has been close to the usual seasonal amount and extremely little of the extra currency called into circulation has come back, perhaps about $50 million, leaving outstanding an extra amount due to extraordinary causes about $300,000,000.

If Fed policymakers were aware that depositor confidence had not been fully restored in January, why, we might ask, did they not take that as a signal that additional action was necessary? To restore confidence, why didn't they initiate a vigorous program of open market purchases? Enough, that is, to convince the doubters that the banking system was safe and that the Fed was prepared to do whatever was necessary to prevent a banking collapse.

Friedman and Schwartz have a different rationale for having recommended that Fed officials should have undertaken a generous program of security purchases – about $1 billion. Their primary concern was the decline in the stock of money and its effect ultimately on output. Since the monetary base had increased, the decline in the money stock was attributable to a decline in the currency–deposit ratio. Substantial purchases were called for to offset the decline in that ratio. But the argument is anachronistic. Knowledge of how the currency–deposit ratio determined the money stock was not available at that time. Meade (1934) and Angell and Ficek (1933) had not made their path-breaking contributions to money supply theory. There is certainly no archival evidence suggesting that at least some reserve bank officials understood the relationship between the currency–deposit ratio, the multiplier, and the stock of money.

As we have attempted to show we need not assume arbitrarily that Fed officials understood the money supply process or even that their primary concern should have been the behavior of the money stock rather than interest rates or other variables. The mere existence of reliable estimates of the amount of nonseasonal hoarding was sufficient to warrant the adoption of an active and vigorous program of open market purchases for the explicit purpose of restoring depositor confidence in the banking system. It would have been an unmistakable signal of how far the Federal Reserve was prepared to go to maintain the liquidity and solvency of the banking system.

8   Summary and conclusions

The principal conclusion to emerge from our description and analysis of the accelerated bank suspensions in November 1930–January 1931 is that there was no national banking crisis. The banking difficulties were region specific, that is, of some local and regional concern but without national importance. There was no panic in the New York money market as revealed by the number of bank suspensions or the behavior of interest rates. Bank debits outside New York City do not show significant effects on final product expenditures except in those areas where the impact of bank suspensions was the highest. Nor would Friedman and Schwartz (1963, p. 313) disagree; they concluded that the first banking crisis "left no clear imprint on the broad economic series" such as personal income and industrial production.

The amount of the money stock between November and January, as we attempted to show, was not exceptionally large compared with prior quarterly changes in 1930 for both M-1 and M-2. Why then, should we attribute special output effects solely to the November–January decline and not to the earlier declines? Friedman and Schwartz have attempted to associate the increase in the currency–deposit ratio solely with the effects of the failure of BUS in December, but we can not reject the hypothesis that the increased demands for currency relative to demand deposits can equally well be explained by the lagged effects of the continued erosion of confidence attributable to the collapse of Caldwell and Company in November, especially since there was the same high concentration of failures in the same three Federal Reserve Districts during both November and December.

The Fed's response during the period of accelerated suspensions and hoarding was successful in warding off a serious disturbance in the New York money market. However, it was not successful in restoring depositor confidence after the crisis had subsided. Increased hoarding was not followed by dishoarding. Depositor confidence was not restored to the pre-crisis level thereby increasing depositor vulnerability to future unanticipated shocks.

The evidence on the causal role of money and bank credit remains highly ambivalent. The historical evidence favors the Friedman and Schwartz interpretation of the banking crisis as a purely autonomous disturbance while the econometric evidence is mixed with no single interpretation of that evidence being preferred to all others.

Table A2.1 *Bank Suspensions and deposits in failed banks by Federal Reserve District, September 1930–January 1931*

Federal Reserve District	Sept. 1930	Oct. 1930	Nov. 1930	Dec. 1930	Jan. 1931
Boston					
No.		1		5	
Deposits*		5		17	
New York					
No.	1			6	2
Deposits	0.2			188	7
Philadelphia					
No.		1		6	3
Deposits		0.8		57	4
Cleveland					
No.	1	1	4	4	7
Deposits	1.7	0.6	1.9	0.8	6
Richmond					
No.	3	2	20	62	18
Deposits	2.6	0.5	27	34	7
Atlanta					
No.	2	1	16	35	36
Deposits	0.4	0.5	31	15	24
Chicago					
No.	23	15	14	53	48
Deposits	12.6	8	3	32	17
St. Louis					
No.	8	8	141	97	47
Deposits	1.7	3.5	133	41	17
Minneapolis					
No.	6	17	27	31	13
Deposits	0.5	2.7	5	8.8	4
Kansas City					
No.	15	14	10	16	16
Deposits	3.2	2.9	5	3.8	4
Dallas					
No.	5	4	3	8	4
Deposits	0.9	0.5	1.8	4	0.6
San Francisco					
No.	2	2	1	5	3
Deposits	0.3	1.3	0.1	5.7	1.4
Totals					
No.	66	66	236	328	197
Deposits	24.1	26.3	207.8	407.1	92

Note: *Deposits in millions.
Source: Board of Governors of the Federal Reserve System, *Federal Reserve Bulletin*, Washington DC, January 1931, p. 77 and November 1930, p. 83.

Table A2.2 Federal Reserve notes in circulation weekly, not seasonally adjusted, October 29, 1930–January 31, 1931 ($m).

	Oct. 29	Nov. 5	Nov. 12	Nov. 19	Nov. 26	Dec. 3	Dec. 10	Dec. 17	Dec. 24	Dec. 31	Jan. 7	Jan. 14	Jan. 21	Jan. 31
Boston	129	130	129	125	128	131	130	133	139	132	127	123	128	127
New York	242	240	233	242	259	271	283	354	400	385	365	327	308	289
Philadelphia	115	118	121	116	123	125	126	130	161	154	146	146	140	139
Cleveland	182	179	185	184	189	190	194	194	204	195	191	186	181	179
Richmond	66	69	69	68	74	73	85	108	108	101	96	90	89	86
Atlanta	117	119	122	124	123	125	124	126	136	134	134	133	135	133
Chicago	147	144	144	142	141	141	142	141	141	139	142	144	143	143
St. Louis	61	62	65	80	84	84	83	84	86	85	84	82	81	80
Minneapolis	49	49	49	48	48	50	50	51	54	54	52	51	50	49
Kansas City	65	66	66	69	66	68	68	69	71	68	68	68	67	66
Dallas	33	34	33	33	32	33	32	32	33	32	31	30	29	28
San Fran.	150	157	156	152	154	156	151	175	189	183	187	174	165	160
Total	1,355	1,367	1,371	1,384	1,422	1,451	1,476	1,596	1,722	1,664	1,625	1,553	1,518	1,478

Source: Commercial and Financial Chronicle.

3   The two banking crises of 1931

No more than two months elapsed between the ending of the first banking crisis and the onset of the second in April 1931. There followed six months of accelerated bank suspensions, deposit losses in failed banks and increased hoarding. Within this six month period we can identify two separate and distinct banking failure episodes: between April and August 563 banks failed with deposits in failed banks totaling $497 million, and between September and October 817 banks suspended with deposits in suspended banks amounting to $747 million. Sixty percent of the 2,293 bank closings in 1931 occurred during the two banking crises. Figure 3.1 shows the geographical density of the failures for the entire year. The amount of hoarding increased about $400 million as measured by Federal Reserve notes in circulation seasonally adjusted in both episodes (see table 3.1). There was a high concentration of bank suspensions in the Chicago Federal Reserve District during the second banking crisis. One-third of all bank suspensions were in the Chicago District and two-thirds of the deposits of failed banks were in the two Districts of Cleveland and Chicago. The source of the initial shock in April we have been unable to identify, but subsequent shocks in June in Chicago and in August in Toledo are easily recognized. We conclude, unlike Friedman and Schwartz, that the second banking crisis was region specific without perceptible nationwide effects.

The onset of the third banking crisis coincides with Britain's departure from the gold standard on September 21, 1931. Bank failures, deposits in failed banks, and increased hoarding immediately accelerated after the British announcement. Nevertheless, we have been unable to find any direct linkage between the gold shock and specific bank suspensions. The external drain of gold was accompanied by an increase in domestic hoarding. We propose to reconstruct the banking crisis of September and October in two separate stages. In the first we employ as our basic unit of analysis each Federal Reserve District for the purpose of revealing the geographical incidence of the crisis. In the second we attempt a select

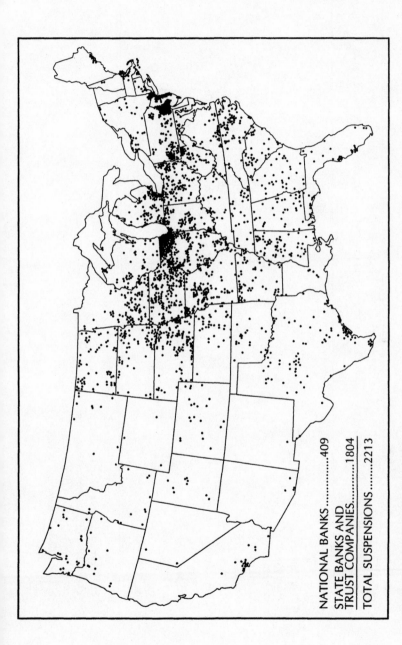

NATIONAL BANKS............409

STATE BANKS AND
TRUST COMPANIES..........1804

TOTAL SUSPENSIONS.......2213

Figure 1.1 Bank suspensions, 1921–9

Source: Board of Governors of the Federal Reserve System. *Bank Suspensions in the United States, 1892–1931,* Vol. 5, Washington, DC, 1933.

Table 3.1 Number of bank suspensions, deposits in closed banks, and increases in hoarding, April–August and September–October 1931 by Federal Reserve District

Federal Reserve District	April–August			September–October		
	No. of bank suspensions (1)	Deposits of failed banks $m. (2)	*Increase in hoarding $m. (3)	No. of bank suspensions (4)	Deposits of failed banks $m. (5)	*Inc. in hoarding $m. (6)
Boston	0	0	0	6	24	6
New York	23	71	143	18	37	76
Philadelphia	18	13	9	59	118	88
Cleveland	55	134	33	72	234	63
Richmond	34	9	−8	89	67	16
Atlanta	14	7	−21	33	7	1
Chicago	194	192	232	204	145	81
St. Louis	26	5	1	82	30	4
Minneapolis	106	21	4	104	25	7
Kansas City	56	17	3	81	18.6	6
Dallas	19	6	1	47	38	12
San Francisco	18	22	17	22	4	33
Totals[1]	563	497	414	817	747	393
Totals[2]	(573)	(496)		(827)	(705)	

Notes: [1] My own estimates from Fed's cumulative total of deposits of failed banks.
[2] Fed's revised estimates of totals for all Districts.
* Federal Reserve notes in circulation seasonally adjusted.
Source: Board of Governors of the Federal Reserve System, *Federal Reserve Bulletin*, 1931.
Commercial and Financial Chronicle, 1931.

microhistory of the crisis by identifying and describing banking disturbances in three cities: Pittsburgh, Philadelphia, and Chicago. We label these banking disturbances mini panics by which we mean a cluster of bank suspensions affecting mainly, though not entirely, a particular kind of bank, namely trust companies, and located in a particular section of the city with deposit losses in each city equal to or less than 8 percent of total deposits in that city. The waves of bank suspensions in these three cities apparently do not conform to the conventional model of a banking panic; that is, a banking panic as an indiscrimate run on banks by all depositors whose confidence in banking institutions has been shattered. During the September–October crisis a contagion of fear did not spread to all banks in any one of the disturbed areas.

A comprehensive narrative of what happened during the two banking crises in 1931 does not exist, at least on a scale comparable to that of the 1930 and 1933 crises. Friedman and Schwartz's account is restricted to what happened at the aggregate level to bank closings, deposit losses, and domestic hoarding. The shock of Britain's departure from gold in September 1931 did not generate any dramatic bank suspensions that had identifiable national significance such as the failure of Caldwell and Company and the Bank of United States in 1930 or the closings of the Michigan banks in March 1933. Moreover, the lion's share of scholarly attention has been reserved for the 1930 crisis because of its allegedly causal role in bringing about the Great Depression.

The reconstruction of the banking crisis of 1931 has important implications for interpreting the Fed's response to gold exports and the acceleration of bank suspensions. The increase in the discount rate in October 1931, for example, has been regarded as an egregious blunder and a major cause of the increase in bank failures and hoarding in October. Moreover, the Fed's failure to prevent the decline in the money stock has been attributed to its failure to offset the increase in the currency–deposit ratio. The harmful effects of the discount rate increase have been exaggerated. Increased bank suspensions and hoarding had preceded the rate increase. The mini panics in Pittsburgh, Philadelphia, and Chicago with their reverberating effects occurred between September 21 and October 9 *before* the discount rate was raised. At least forty-two banks in these three cities suspended operations with unrevised deposit losses totalling $165 million. Sixty percent of the increase in hoarding occurred between September 16 and October 7. The discount rate increase played no causal role in initiating the banking crisis. The Fed's failure to have prevented the decline in the money stock was due less to ineptitude than to economists' lack of knowledge of how the currency–deposit ratio affects the multiplier. The first articles incorporating the currency–deposit ratio into the multiplier mechanism appeared in 1933 and 1934, too late to have been known to Reserve Bank officials.

President Hoover assumed responsibility for managing the impending banking crisis by announcing on October 7, two days before the New York Fed increased the discount rate, a bold program for providing liquidity to troubled banks by the creation of a National Credit Corporation. The contribution of Hoover's announcement to the restoration of confidence in the banking system and to the ending of the panic has largely been ignored.

The first section of this chapter examines the second banking crisis from April to August. The second describes the third banking crisis and contrasts the two. The mini banking panics in Pittsburgh, Philadelphia, and Chicago are described in the third. The fourth section reevaluates the Fed's response to the banking crisis, and the role of the National Credit Corporation created at the request of President Hoover. Section 5 asks whether there was anything special about the 1931 banking crisis. Section 6 reevaluates the role of the 1931 crisis in contributing to the Great Depression. A summary and conclusions follow.

1   The region specific second banking crisis: April–August 1931

According to Friedman and Schwartz (1963) the second banking crisis began in March 1931 and ended in August, but April is probably the preferred month for pinpointing the onset of the second crisis. Official estimates show currency in circulation seasonally adjusted beginning to increase only in April.

Table 3.1 shows the number of bank suspensions, deposits of closed banks, and increases in hoarding for the two periods April–August and September–October for each of the twelve Federal Reserve Districts and table 3.2 shows bank suspensions, deposits in failed banks and currency in circulation monthly for 1931. I have constructed monthly estimates for deposits in failed banks. In February 1932 the Fed revised its monthly estimates for bank suspensions and seasonally unadjusted deposits in closed banks for member and nonmember banks for 1931 and annual estimates by Federal Reserve District. The Fed never revised its previously published monthly estimates by Federal Reserve District for 1931. The discrepancy between the revised annual and unrevised monthly totals for the year was substantial, $1,690 million and $2,009 million respectively, a difference of more than $300 million.

I concluded that the disparity was too wide to warrant the use of unrevised current monthly estimates of deposit losses. Fortunately, the *Federal Reserve Bulletin* after February 1932 also contained estimates

Table 3.2 *Number of bank suspensions, deposits in failed banks and currency in circulation variously defined monthly, 1931*

Month	Number of bank suspensions	Deposits of failed banks $m (revised by Fed '32)	Currency in circulation[1]	Federal reserve notes $m[2]
January	198	76	4,425	1,521
February	76	35	4,370	1,484
March	86	34	4,355	1,486
April	64	42	4,405	1,560
May	91	43	4,445	1,611
June	167	190	4,525	1,703
July	93	41	4,595	1,766
August	158	180	4,705	1,908
September	305	234	4,820	2,025
October	522	471	5,130	2,295
November	175	68	5,140	2,388
December	353	277	5,125	2,397
TOTALS	2,288	1,691		

[1] Monthly averages of daily figures, seasonally adjusted.
[2] Seasonally adjusted, my estimate. Monthly averages of daily figures.
Sources: Board of Governors of the Federal Reserve System,
Banking and Monetary Statistics, Washington DC (August 1976), pp. 412, 414.
Federal Reserve Bulletin, September 1937, Washington DC, pp. 907, 909.

cumulatively for January to the current month through December. The cumulative totals did include revisions of the previous month's estimates of both bank suspensions and deposits of failed banks. Deposits of failed banks in the current month were entered either at the date of suspension, if known, or the nearest call date. As data on deposits at date of suspension became available, the cumulative deposit totals were revised, but no revisions were made in the previous month's estimate for each Federal Reserve District. Using data on the cumulative total in the preceding month and the reported data in the current month, I constructed a monthly series for deposits in failed banks backward from December to January (see footnote for details of how the series was constructed and appendix 3.3 for the estimates monthly for 1931).[1] These estimates appear in table 3.1. The discrepancy between the Fed's 1932 revised annual estimate ($1,691 million) and the Fed's cumulative total estimates for January–December ($1,787 million) was reduced by two-thirds. The discrepancy between my monthly estimates and the Fed's 1932 revised estimates vanishes for the April–August period and is $40 million for the September–October period. Table 3.2 provides the Fed's revised estimates monthly for bank suspensions and deposits of failed banks as well as estimates of Federal Reserve notes in circulation seasonally adjusted.

Table 3.1 shows that between April and August 563 banks failed with deposits in failed banks amounting to $497 million. Three-quarters of all bank suspensions were located in the Federal Reserve Districts of Chicago, Minneapolis, Cleveland, and Kansas City.

More than one-third of all bank suspensions were in the Chicago

[1] Specifically, to obtain a monthly estimate for June, for example, I added the reported cumulative total for January–May and reported deposits in failed banks for June and then subtracted from the reported cumulative total. One-half of the difference was added to or subtracted from the reported June estimate; the other half was used to adjust the January–May cumulative total. I began with December and adjusted the monthly estimates back to January. The adjustment proportion – one-half – was arbitrary. But one can argue plausibly that the current month's reported estimate of deposit losses is likely to have been derived from deposits at prior call dates since information would not always be available immediately of deposit losses at time of closure. Why the Fed did not revise the previous month's estimate when new information became available remains a mystery. Instead they revised the cumulative total from January to the current month without any explanation.

The discrepancy between the Fed's cumulative totals and the sum of the Fed's monthly estimates by District was $52 million for April–August and $75 million for September–October. In the April–August period 56 percent of the discrepancy is attributable to three Federal Reserve Districts: New York, Chicago, and Cleveland. In the September–October period, two-thirds of the discrepancy occurs in the Chicago and Cleveland Districts, with the Cleveland District accounting for one-half of the discrepancy. Deposit losses in the Cleveland Districts exceeded those of all other Districts.

District with nearly 200 closed banks. Two of the four Districts – Chicago and Cleveland – had two-thirds of the deposits of suspended banks. Banking panics in Toledo, Ohio and Chicago, Illinois explain three-fourths and one-third respectively of deposit losses in the Cleveland and Chicago Federal Reserve Districts. Four of Toledo's nine banks had failed on August 17 with deposit losses totalling over $80 million deactivating funds of at least 150,000 depositors. The third largest bank in Toledo with deposits of more than $20 million – Security Home Trust – failed on June 17 at which time three other large banks announced a sixty-day withdrawal requirement for savings deposits. Three of the four banks that failed on August 17 were the same banks that had initiated the withdrawal request sixty days earlier.

No other urban banking panic in the whole of 1931 surpassed that of Toledo if measured either by deposit losses of failed banks or percentage of deposit losses in failed banks to total deposits within the city. The impact of deposit losses of this magnitude on depositor confidence both in Ohio and in the Cleveland Federal Reserve District can hardly be overestimated and cannot be confined solely to the month of August. As we shall see, the incidence of deposit losses in the Cleveland District remained high in September and October as well.

In June a mini banking crisis erupted and swept away more than thirty banks in Chicago with unrevised deposit losses close to $60 million. The mini panic in June was preceded by a sequence of failures in March and April. On March 30, for example, three suburban banks failed to open with deposits of over $5 million. Between April 1 and 16, seven more Chicago banks suspended operations with deposits of $13.5 million.

The vulnerability of Chicago banks to failure was idiosyncratic. No other city of the same size and financial importance faced identical growth constraints imposed by legislative fiat. In 1923 the Illinois legislature passed an act to prohibit the operation of branches within the state, thereby confining the growth of banking services within the city of Chicago in areas recently developed to newly established independent banks. Population in the outlying suburbs had increased by more than 70 percent, from 1,552,000 to 2,670,000 from 1917 to 1927. In 1914 Chicago had some sixty-six banks in outlying areas of the city. By 1928 the number had increased by almost five-fold to 337!

The expansion of the number of independent banks per se does not imply necessarily increased risk of failure. It was the reasons for the growth that imparted the vulnerability to failure. According to James (1938, p. 953) this increase in the number of banks in outlying areas was the "the outgrowth of the real estate boom" between 1922 and 1926.

Promoters of real estate developments needed a source of funds to finance mortgages which they found in the chartering of new and independent banks. During the real estate boom land values had soared, and mortgages became valued securities in the portfolio of earning assets. Banks also had issued real estate mortgage bonds and sold them with an understanding they would repurchase them if the sellers became dissatisfied, a provision the banks would later regret. By the end of 1930 many of these banks in outlying areas were in "dire distress." The value of real estate assets plummeted and dissatisfied holders of mortgage bonds attempted to sell them back to the banks from which they were purchased.

Loop banks stopped repurchasing mortgage bonds in the spring of 1931. When the Foreman Group of banks hesitated, aggregate deposits of these banks began to fall, and a run on the Group occurred which eventually engulfed as many as thirty banks with deposits of more than $60 million between June 8 and June 11. On June 8 the Foreman Group merged with First National of Chicago. On the same day six banks allied with Foreman in outlying areas were closed voluntarily. On June 9, twelve banks in the Bain chain of banks suspended with $16 million of deposits, and on June 10 six more outlying banks closed with combined deposits of nearly $20 million, two of which were affiliated with the Foreman banks.

Table 3.3 reveals the sharp increase in postal savings deposits in the city of Chicago during the month of June, a good proxy for the state of public confidence in Chicago banks, a 40 percent increase over the preceding month. Esbitt (1986, p. 460) showed that Chicago banks which failed in 1931 were plagued by poor management. He used as key indicators of poor management of failed banks relative to banks that did not fail the amount of secondary reserves, real estate loans, amount of fixed assets, and amount of earned capital. Banks that failed held fewer secondary reserves, more real estate loans, more fixed assets, and lower levels of earned capital than non-failing banks.

Each succeeding reverberating shock took its toll on banks in the outlying Chicago area, but the vulnerability to succeeding shocks had its origins in the real estate boom in the mid twenties and its subsequent collapse.

Table 3.1 reveals that the increase in hoarding as proxied by Federal Reserve notes in circulation seasonally adjusted was highly concentrated in four of the twelve Federal Reserve Districts with the Chicago District bearing the brunt of the banking crisis. Column 3 shows the net change in hoarding between April and August. In seven Districts there was either little or no change or a decrease in hoarding. There was a slight

Table 3.3   *Postal savings account balances monthly: Chicago, June 1930–October 1931 (in thousands)*

Month	Amount	Change
June 1930	4,053	−4
August 1930	4,803	+750
September 1930	5,205	+402
October 1930	5,500	+295
November 1930	5,785	+285
December 1930	6,190	+405
January 1931	7,592	+1,402
February 1931	8,564	+972
March 1931	9,173	+609
April 1931	11,968	+2,795
May 1931	13,290	+1,322
June 1931	18,860	+5,570
July 1931	22,281	+3,421
August 1931	24,604	+2,323
September 1931	28,981	+4,377
October 1931 (first 20 days)	33,000	+4,019

Source: Chicago Tribune, Thursday, October 29, 1931, p. 23.

increase in Kansas City and Minneapolis even though the rate of bank suspensions was high in both Districts, and little change in Dallas. There was a decrease in Richmond and Atlanta. In only two, New York and Chicago, was there any substantial increase and more than one-half was in the Chicago District.

The relatively large increase in Federal Reserve notes in circulation in the New York District between April and August requires some explanation. There was no serious disturbance in the New York money market. The increase in hoarding was too large to be explained solely by the number of bank suspensions and deposits in suspended banks. Twenty-three banks failed with deposit losses of $81 million. Yet, the increase in hoarding amounted to $143 million. Some of the increase might be attributed to currency exports resulting from the banking crisis in Germany and Austria in July and August 1931 and some to the rundown of interbank deposits as banks outside New York City liquidated their balances for the purpose of restoring liquidity. Interbank deposits at weekly reporting member banks in New York City declined approximately $200 million between March and August.

Unlike pre-Great Depression banking crises, the New York money market was not a primary source of disturbances during the second banking crisis. The crisis had originated elsewhere. The New York market absorbed without dire consequences the demand for funds generated by the loss of depositor confidence in the interior of the country.

The internal drain of currency was not accompanied, however, by an external drain between April and August. In fact, these five months are characterized by a flood of gold imports amounting to $300 million to which the Fed responded by reducing the buying rate on acceptances from $1\frac{1}{2}$ percent on April 22 to 1 percent in the second week of May. Presumably, the decrease was to aid Britain in protecting her gold reserve. Financial unrest in Europe was at least partially responsible for the influx of gold. Banking troubles in Austria and Germany during May, June, and July induced some investors to seek a safe haven for their funds in the US. Gold imports obviated the need to offset deliberately the effects of the hoarding increase. Federal Reserve officials were able to meet the internal drain passively by allowing gold imports to exert their full effects on reserve deposits.

From our examination of the second banking crisis we conclude that there was no geographically diffused nationwide banking crisis between April and August 1931. Banking suspensions were centered in a relatively few Federal Reserve Districts. The banking crisis was largely a region specific phenomenon; it had not yet become a full-fledged national crisis.

Wigmore (1985, p. 203) has denied that there was any banking crisis during the first six months of 1931. He stated: "Deposits in closed banks were not growing, and runs on banks were few." The only problem, he averred, was the low level of short-term interest rates which was making it difficult to make a profit on short-run deposits. Wigmore may have gone too far in denying the existence of a banking crisis. There was a full-scale panic in Toledo in August and a mini panic in Chicago in June but, perhaps, he only meant a crisis national in scope. The second banking crisis was a prelude to one far more serious and nationwide in scope. Nevertheless, bank failures remained high in both the Chicago and Cleveland Federal Reserve Districts.

2   The third banking crisis: September–October 1931 – two crises contrasted

The third banking crisis was coincident with the external shock; that is, Britain's announcement on September 21 that the pound would no longer be convertible into gold at a fixed parity. The number of bank suspensions, deposits in failed banks, and domestic hoarding accelerated immediately. The crisis was well under way, however, before the New York Fed requested and received approval from the Federal Reserve Board to increase the discount rate two and a half weeks later on October 9. Friedman and Schwartz (1963) state that the crisis began in September and ended in December. Nevertheless, there are good reasons for preferring October to December as the terminal date: (1) both the number of suspensions and deposits of closed banks fell off sharply in November, (2) there was a marked deceleration of hoarding in November and December, and (3) even though bank suspensions and deposits in failed banks accelerated in December, depositor confidence increased, currency in circulation declined.

The deceleration of hoarding in November and December meant that public distrust of the banking system had stabilized. The panic was over. Nevertheless, an important caveat attaches to this inference. The panic may have subsided, but there was no substantial return flow of currency to the banking system, a significant fact to which we will refer later in considering whether or not banking crises of the Great Depression were different in character from other banking panics in US history.

To reveal the intensity of the crisis after Britain abandoned gold on September 21 we will compare the behavior of the three indicators over the two periods April–August and September–October. Data for both September and October distort the impact of the external shock of Britain's abandonment of gold, for it is only the last nine days of September that are relevant. But this is unavoidable. No data exist on weekly bank suspensions or deposits in failed banks. We do have data, however, on weekly movements in Federal Reserve notes by District not seasonally adjusted. What those data reveal is that 67 percent of the increase in Federal Reserve notes in circulation in September took place during the last two weeks of September, the third week overlapping Britain's decision to suspend gold convertibility.

It is clear from table 3.1 that both the number of suspensions and deposits of failed banks and hoarding accelerated sharply in September and October compared with the preceding five months. However, the share of deposits in closed banks in three Districts – Chicago, Cleveland, and Philadelphia – remained the same between the two periods at approximately 68 percent. However, the distribution of deposits between the three Districts changed. The decline in Chicago's share was offset by increases in both Cleveland and Philadelphia. The increase in hoarding was about the same in the two periods. But the increase occurred over a two month period (September–October) instead of five (April–August), indicative of the seriousness of the September–October banking crisis.

A comparison of the two periods has revealed a sharp acceleration of the amount of bank suspensions, deposits in failed banks, and domestic hoarding in the September–October period. Moreover, the banking crisis changed its character from primarily region specific to nationwide in scope with unequal incidence among the regions. The largest concentration of deposits in failed banks in October, the first full month of the crisis, was in the Cleveland District with $178 million or one-third of total deposits of failed banks. The Philadelphia District was second with $96 million.

Twenty-four banks suspended operations in Ohio (the Cleveland District) in October, but only five accounted for roughly 88 percent of deposits of suspended banks. The three largest banks in Youngstown, Ohio closed on October 15 with deposits as of the latest reporting date of $64 million. On October 22 the largest bank in Canton, Ohio with deposits of $20 million closed its doors, and on October 31 the largest bank in Dayton with $31 million ceased operations.

Nineteen banks failed in West Virginia in the ten day period from October 13 to October 22 most of which had deposits of less than $1 million. The failed banks in West Virginia accounted for more than 50 percent of the suspended banks in the Richmond District. Sixteen banks failed in Missouri between October 15 and 26.

Of the more than 101 failures identified by bank in the *Commercial and Financial Chronicle* in October, forty occurred during the first week, seventeen in the second week, and forty-four in the third week. The first and third weeks witnessed the highest failure rates. The *Chronicle* is a major source of individual bank failures for the country as a whole. Their list of bank suspensions represents a little over 21 percent of total suspensions in October. Urban coverage is more complete than rural. However, number of suspensions is less important than the amount of deposits in failed banks which, as we have attempted to show, covers a sizeable proportion of total deposits.

I have also been able to identify a small number of cities outside Pittsburgh, Chicago, and Philadelphia with multibank suspensions. I have referred to the failure of three Youngstown, Ohio banks on October 15. Three Parkersburg, West Virginia banks failed on November 2 and 3. Three banks closed in Evansville, Indiana on October 22. Four New York City banks were closed by the Superintendent of Banking on October 16 with deposits of $31 million. Two national banks suspended in Morgantown, West Virginia on October 13; two in Brickham, West Virginia on October 16; two banks in Slater, Missouri on October 26; two banks in Buchanan, Michigan on October 17. This list is not complete, but it would not be imprudent to conclude that multibank failures within one town or city within a one week interval were not numerous.

Our description of what happened has turned up discrepancies between the three basic measures of the September–October banking crisis: the number of bank suspensions, the amount of deposits in failed banks, and changes in the amount of hoarding. Of the three, the number of bank suspensions is perhaps the least informative unless supplemented by additional data on geographical incidence and size distribution of closed banks. From the number of bank suspensions alone we can infer little or nothing about either the seriousness or the nature of the difficulties of the banking industry as a whole. Mass exodus from the banking industry is, of course, indicative of a problem, but whether that problem is of purely local or national concern cannot be assumed. We cannot infer a general loss of depositor confidence in the banking system. For example, between 1921 and 1929 bank suspensions averaged 635 a year. Yet, there was no national banking panic and no increase in hoarding.

The amount of deposits in failed banks is perhaps a better measure of the economic burden of bank suspensions. If, like Friedman and Schwartz, we regard the money stock effects of bank closures on economic activity as critical, then deposits of failed banks are far more important than mere numbers of bank failures. Deposits in closed banks is also a good proxy for the curtailment of checking account services.

For the purpose of identifying depositor unrest, changes in the amount of currency holdings of the banks and the public are far more revealing than either the amount of deposits in failed banks or the number of bank suspensions.

A comparison of relative District rankings in September–October by number of suspensions, deposits in failed banks, and changes in Federal Reserve notes in circulation reveals the following results:

1 The correlation is very close in each District between the amount of deposits in failed banks and the increase in Federal Reserve notes in circulation. Cleveland was first in amount of deposits in failed banks and third in the increase in notes in circulation not seasonally adjusted. Philadelphia was third in deposits of failed banks and second in the increase in notes in circulation. Chicago was second and fourth respectively. The only significant aberration was New York – sixth and first respectively. The rank correlation coefficient is 0.6924.

2 The number of suspensions correlates poorly with the increase in notes in circulation. Apparently it is not the number of suspensions that drives the increase in hoarding so much as the amount of

deposits in failed banks. Philadelphia, for example, ranked seventh in number of suspensions but second in the amount of notes in circulation. New York was first along with Philadelphia in the increase in hoarding but almost last (eleventh) in the number of bank suspensions. The rank correlation coefficient is −0.1013.

3 The rank correlation coefficient for the number of bank suspensions and the amount of deposits in failed banks is 0.423.

David Wheelock (1994) has suggested that the variables of interest should be the suspension rate; that is, suspensions divided by operating banks and the ratio of deposits rather than simply the number of suspensions and the amount of deposits in suspended banks. A given number of bank suspensions might induce very different amounts of hoarding depending on whether or not the number of suspensions represented a high proportion of a region's banks. Regrettably the experiment cannot be carried out. The total number of operating banks and total deposits by Federal Reserve District do not exist on a monthly basis; the data are only available on call dates for all banks.

What this evidence tells us is that the relationship between hoarding and bank suspensions is more complex than it may first appear. Hoarding cannot be explained solely by the number of bank suspensions. As we have stated bank failures were abnormally high in the 1920s yet there was no loss of depositor confidence nor any decrease in the money stock. Moreover, when the bank failure rate subsided in June and November 1931 there was no significant reduction in the amount of Federal Reserve notes in circulation. The decrease in bank suspensions did not restore depositor confidence. The total number of bank closings fell from 522 in October to 175 in November, yet depositor confidence was not restored. Notes in circulation declined by a mere $1.3 million from $2,447 million to $2,445 million. In the Chicago District, for example, while the number of suspensions in October increased by only ten from ninety-seven to 107, notes in circulation increased by $35 million.

Bank suspensions can sometimes trigger a contagion of fear that induces hoarding which, in turn, may lead to more bank suspensions. The relationship is likely to be one of mutual causality and interdependence that reaches it zenith during a national banking crisis.

The number of bank suspensions is probably not as important as bank size and the amount of deposits in suspended banks in inducing depositor distrust. As we have seen the amount of deposits in closed banks correlates more closely with notes in circulation than does the number of bank suspensions. The number of bank failures, therefore, is not a reliable indicator of depositor distrust.

The relationship between deposits in failed banks and hoarding did not hold for the New York District. Hoarding in the New York District is inexplicable in terms of what was happening solely within the District. In October notes in circulation not seasonally adjusted increased by $92 million, exceeded only by the $100 million increase in the Philadelphia District. The number of suspensions in the Philadelphia District increased from twelve to forty-seven between September and October and deposits in failed banks from $22 million to $96 million. As we shall see in the next section, there was a mini banking panic in Philadelphia and good reason for the increase in hoarding. But there was no banking crisis in the New York money market. The number of suspensions in the District increased from seven to eleven and deposits in failed banks from $8 million to $32 million. The increase in notes in circulation of $92 million cannot be explained by depositor distrust within the District. Vault cash of New York reporting member banks shows virtually no increase between September 29 and November 4. That is not what we would have expected if there had been runs on New York banks. Moreover, data for select banks and financial institutions in New York City show net receipts of currency from Europe exceeded by $8.5 million shipments to Europe. I suspect currency outflows for *all* New York City banks were not reported and account for some, though how much we will never know, of the $92 million increase in hoarding.

The other remaining possibility is the withdrawal of deposits by interior banks from New York City banks in exchange for currency. Interbank deposits at weekly reporting member banks in New York City declined from $1,204 million on September 30 to $956 million on October 28 (Wednesday figures), a decline of approximately $250 million. There was a decline of $149 million during the first week of October and another $50 million in the second and third weeks when the crisis in the rest of the country was at its peak. It is reasonable to assume that the withdrawal of interbank deposits was made to obtain currency.

A review of the data on bank suspensions, deposits in failed banks, and domestic hoarding by Federal Reserve District and by state has revealed the following:

1   A full-fledged nationwide banking crisis erupted when Britain announced its departure from gold convertibility on September 21, 1931. Prior to that date bank suspensions during the five-month period from April through August had been region specific with the Chicago District the focus of banking unrest.

2 Three Federal Reserve Districts: Chicago, Philadelphia, and Cleveland accounted for nearly two-thirds of the deposits of suspended banks in September and October.
3 The same three Districts can explain at least one-half of the increase in domestic hoarding.
4 There was no crisis in the New York Federal Reserve District including New York City measured by either the number of suspensions or deposits in failed banks, though deposits in closed banks in New York were larger than in six other Districts.
5 The increase in Federal Reserve notes in circulation in the New York District, which was equal to that of Philadelphia, is not a reliable indicator of depositor distrust within the District since some of the notes were either shipped abroad or sent to other District commercial banks in exchange for withdrawal of interbank deposits.

Now we turn to the microhistory of the mini panics in Chicago, Philadelphia, and Pittsburgh.

3   Mini panics in Philadelphia, Pittsburgh, and Chicago

In September and October two out of every three dollars of deposits in suspended banks were in the three Federal Reserve Districts of Philadelphia, Cleveland, and Chicago. Together these three Districts accounted for 40 percent of bank failures in these two months. They also were responsible for 60 percent of the increase in Federal Reserve notes in circulation.

We may be able to gain valuable insight into what happened in each of the three Districts by reconstructing the mini panics that occurred in a leading city in each District: Philadelphia in the Philadelphia District, Pittsburgh in the Cleveland District, and Chicago in the Chicago District. To repeat, by a mini panic I mean a cluster of bank failures affecting mainly, though not entirely, smaller banks in a particular city where deposit losses equal less than 8 percent of total deposits of banks in each city and where bank runs did not indiscriminately engulf all banks in a city. Information about the course of the mini panic in each large city is far more accessible than what is available for bank closings in rural areas.

The primary source materials for the reconstruction of the mini panics are local and national newspapers and operations and balance sheet data for individual suspended banks compiled by state and federal regulatory authorities wherever available. Ideally both kinds of information form the basis for the construction of a detailed narrative of what happened during the panics in each of the three cities. The first task of the historian of banking panics is to locate where the suspensions occurred, the names of the suspended banks and to trace the course of the panic, that is, who initiated the panic and how the panic spread throughout a given geographical area. It is equally important to identify the proximate cause of a bank's collapse: a run on the bank or a closure with no bank run at the initiative of the bank's directors or supervisory authority due to a condition of insolvency. The second task is to discern the financial state of each of the banks at the time of closure. But that depends on the accessibility of data.

Neither of the two tasks has hitherto been attempted for the two banking crises of 1931. However, James (1938) has provided a narrative of sorts of the banking panics in the city of Chicago in June and in September–October 1931. Esbitt (1986) drew a sample of 101 state-chartered Chicago banks having assets of less than $20 million as of December 1927 including some of the banks that failed in 1930, 1931, and 1932 and compared the banks that failed in those years with those that did not fail. But no similar exercise has been attempted for Philadelphia or Pittsburgh banks. Such studies constitute an agenda for future research and will not be attempted here.

Our main focus will be to identify where the panic occurred and the number and deposits of the suspended banks. Little additional information is provided in the newspaper sources. At the height of the panic within the city, editors were generally reluctant to make a dramatic front page display for fear of exacerbating depositor unrest. Speculation about the probable course of the panic was minimal. All too frequently no reasons were given for bank closures especially if the banks were located on the periphery of the city. Surprisingly, the task of reconstructing what happened during the mini panics in Chicago, Philadelphia, and Pittsburgh has been hampered by a dearth of information. And that probably accounts for our general lack of knowledge of what happened throughout the country during the banking crises.

The first question we must address is how important were the suspensions in the three cities compared with suspensions in the entire District. Eleven Pittsburgh banks suspended during the last nine days of September with an estimated $67 million of deposits. These estimates include deposits at the last reporting date and not deposits at the time of suspension. Therefore, they are not strictly comparable with our revised monthly totals for each District. Nevertheless, we can obtain some idea of their significance by comparing deposit losses in these eleven Pittsburgh banks with the Fed's unrevised September estimates for the Cleveland District. The Pittsburgh failures represented one-half of the bank closings in the Cleveland District for September and 84 percent of the deposits in closed banks.

Twenty banks failed in the city of Philadelphia in October which constituted 43 percent of the failures in the Philadelphia District but over 74 percent of the deposits of failed banks in the District. Eleven banks failed in the Chicago District with total deposits of at least $22 million between September 23 and October 30. Deposits of failed banks in Chicago in September represented 11 percent of total deposits in failed banks in the District and in October 16 percent. The bank failures in Illinois were much higher. Since there are sizeable errors in the unrevised current estimates of deposits in failed banks for each Federal Reserve District and especially the Chicago and Cleveland Districts not too much significance can be attached to the specific numbers. Nevertheless, the estimates do reveal the relative importance of deposit losses in these three key cities.

To gauge how extensive the banking crises were in Pittsburgh, Philadelphia, and Chicago, we describe briefly the market structure of banking in the three cities. Philadelphia had a total of eighty-three commercial and savings banks and trust companies in 1931 as listed in *Rand McNally's Bankers' Directory* (1931) with total deposits amounting to nearly $2 billion. Of these eighty-three banks the top ten held more than 70 percent of total deposits. One-half of the banks had deposits below $5 million with 3.1 percent of total deposits. Sixty-five percent of the banks each had deposits of less than $10 million. Their cumulative share of total deposits was less than 10 percent.

During October twenty banks closed, 24 percent of the total number of banks in Philadelphia. However, these twenty banks had deposits equal only to 3.2 percent of total deposits in Philadelphia banks. Eleven of the suspended banks represented 65 percent of the bank suspensions in Philadelphia but only 20 percent of the deposits in failed banks. Four banks accounted for 70 percent of deposits in suspended banks. However, the largest of the four sustained one-half of the deposit losses.

Pittsburgh with a population of 670,000 in 1931 had sixty-four bank and trust companies. Sixty percent of deposits were concentrated in seven banks with deposits in each bank amounting to more than $50 million. Thirty-five percent of the banks had deposits less than $2.5 million or 2.7 percent of total deposits of Pittsburgh banks. Over one-half of the banks had deposits of less than $5 million (8 percent of total deposits). Of the eleven of the sixteen failures that can be identified from *Rand-McNally's Directory* (1931), nine had deposits of less than $6 million. One ranked in the top seven by size of deposits with deposits of more than $50 million; the other bank ranked tenth with deposits of $16 million.

There were more than 300 banks in the city of Chicago at the end of 1930 with total deposits of more than $2 billion. Deposit losses in June in the failed banks in the Chicago District amounted to 64 percent of total losses for the entire country. The September–October crisis in Chicago was mild. Nevertheless, the number of failures was exceeded only by suspensions in Philadelphia and Pittsburgh.

Philadelphia

During the week beginning September 29, six banks closed located mainly in northeast Philadelphia, five of which were trust companies; their combined deposits amounted to $9 million. The Philadelphia Clearing House Association ordered all banks to enforce the legal time delay of sixty days in withdrawing time and savings deposits. The officers of the Clearing House gave as their reason, to counteract the spread of a "form of hysteria" within the city, the closing of the six banks in northeast Philadelphia. According to an editorial in the *Philadelphia Inquirer* on October 5, there was a growing disposition to withdraw savings deposits, receive cash, and place it in safe deposit boxes. For the week beginning October 5, six more trust companies failed with deposits equal to $35.6 million, the largest of the five was Franklin Trust with total deposits of $23 million, the deposits of which had fallen from $39 million in December 1930 to $23 million in October 1931. On October 7 civic and business leaders urged Philadelphians to stop hoarding, a request that was repeated by George Norris, Governor of the Federal Reserve Bank of Philadelphia. The Federal Reserve Bank of Philadelphia was well informed about the amount of the increase in hoarding and the danger to the safety of the banking system, but the Bank was powerless to act on its own initiative to control hoarding. There were only five additional failures in October with deposits totalling over $21.4 million. By then the mini panic had subsided but without any reduction in notes in circulation.

What can we conclude from the Philadelphia experience? There was a mini panic in Philadelphia confined almost exclusively to trust companies, and small ones at that, with the only exception being Franklin Trust with $23 million of deposits. The larger Philadelphia banks were unaffected, though that does not mean that they did not experience some deposit withdrawals. The contagion of fear simply did not spread to the very largest banks. In fact, seven of the larger and stronger banks announced on Wednesday, October 14 that they would do whatever was necessary to prevent the Integrity Trust Company with $61 million of deposits from failing, a good indication of the magnitude of the bank failure problem in Philadelphia.

All of the banks that failed were not members of the Federal Reserve and did not have access to the discount window. The Federal Reserve Bank of Philadelphia was precluded from coming to their assistance and was defenseless in the face of the bank runs, other than to guarantee assistance to member banks that were solvent and had the requisite paper to discount. At least three of the closed banks had suffered a persistent seepage of deposits since December 1930. Deposits had fallen from $2.4 million to $800,000 in Jefferson Title and Trust; from $39 million to $23 million in Franklin Trust, and from $7.9 million to $4.6 million in County Trust. Banks weakened by such substantial deposit losses over an extended period of time were simply in no condition to forestall the shock of a depositor run.

Twenty Philadelphia banks closed their doors in October with deposits of $81 million, only one of which was not a trust company. Bank failures in Philadelphia constituted 36 percent of the failures in October in the Philadelphia District and 60 percent of the deposits of failed banks.

Pittsburgh

On Monday, September 21 one of the largest banks in Pittsburgh, the Bank of Pittsburgh, with 17,000 depositors closed voluntarily, the alleged reason being the steady withdrawal of deposits by correspondent banks in other sections of the country. As of July 3 its assets amounted to $53 million and deposits of $47 million. On the same day, two smaller banks closely associated with the Bank of Pittsburgh suspended with deposits of $7 million. Continued withdrawals through the remainder of the week led to the closing of three trust companies on Thursday and Friday with deposits of $3 million. Four more banks closed on Saturday. Total deposits of the ten suspended banks amounted to roughly $63 million within one week. Considering that the Cleveland District had an unrevised total of $80 million of deposits in failed banks in September, bank suspensions in Pittsburgh in that one week accounted for as much as 80 percent of the total. Six of the ten were trust companies.

In October two national banks, one state bank, and one private bank closed with deposits of over $22 million. Five banks closed in Washington County contiguous to Pittsburgh with deposits of $9.1 million. Deposits of failed banks for the two week period amounted to $85 million. The failure of the Bank of Pittsburgh had triggered at least fifteen additional suspensions accounting for a sizeable portion of the losses in September and October in the Cleveland District.

Britain suspended gold payments on September 21, the same day that the Bank of Pittsburgh closed. The two events were not related. Moreover, bank suspensions in Pittsburgh did not represent a general erosion of confidence in all Pittsburgh banks. The larger banks were unscathed. There was no dramatic banking panic in Pittsburgh discernible from newspaper accounts, though the failure of the Bank of Pittsburgh received front page coverage.

What we have learned from the Pennsylvania experience is the constrained nature of the panics in Pittsburgh and Philadelphia. The number of suspended banks in both cities was confined mainly to nonmember banks and to trust companies whose deposits were largely savings deposits. The deposit totals for suspended banks, however, are inflated by two outliers: The Bank of Pittsburgh with deposits of $47 million, 67 percent of the deposits of the seventeen suspended Pittsburgh banks, and the Franklin Trust with 44 percent of the deposits of the suspended banks in Philadelphia.

Chicago

The number of bank closings in October in the Chicago Federal Reserve District was only 10 percent greater than in the previous month. But bank suspensions in the Chicago District still remained a significant share of the total – 30 percent in September and 20 percent in October. Nevertheless, the amount of deposits in suspended banks increased from $58 million in September to $96 million in October. The increase in hoarding in October was the fourth largest among the twelve Reserve Districts.

Between September 23 and October 30, eleven banks closed their doors in the city of Chicago with deposits of at least $25 million. Each of the suspended banks had deposits of less than $5 million. The failures were confined almost entirely to the outlying area of the city. No Loop banks were affected and, according to James (1938), bank runs were limited to those banks that were known to be weak. He stated that in the case of earlier runs (before June 1932): "the crowds had been drawn from a particular locality or a special group: this time [June 1932] people from all parts of the city seemed to converge on the Loop in hysterical fear and anxiety." In October, thirty-two banks failed in the State of Illinois with $19 million of deposits. But only seven of those were located in the city. In September, twenty-six banks suspended in Illinois with deposits of $22 million, only four of which were Chicago banks.

It is clear that the crisis in September–October did not match the June crisis in severity when thirty banks had failed. Hoarding was nevertheless exacerbated even though the number of bank closings was relatively small.

There is a reliable measure of hoarding in the city of Chicago monthly from March 1930 to October 1931. We have data on postal savings deposits for banks in Chicago. Table 3.3 shows the sharp increase in June 1931 indicative of the banking crisis during that month. There was a decline in July and August and a substantial increase in September and October. The extent of the increase is readily discernible by comparing the increases in September and October 1931 with similar figures for 1930. The relatively small number of failures in the city of Chicago belies the severity of the mini panic, if measured by the increase in hoarding. Table 3.3 reveals that the banking situation in June was worse than it was in September and October.

We have been able to locate successfully the major centers of disturbance during the September–October banking panic. Multibank failures in three large cities – Pittsburgh, Philadelphia, and Chicago – explain a preponderant amount of the deposits in suspended banks in their affiliated Federal Reserve Districts – especially Cleveland and Philadelphia; less so in Chicago. As far as I have been able to determine, no other US city endured a banking crisis of equal severity in September and October.

Bank suspensions in each of the three cities were associated with a panic-generated withdrawal of funds by depositors. In two of the three, Chicago and Philadelphia, the impact was felt first by banks located on the cities' outskirts. In Pittsburgh the voluntary closing of one of the larger intermediate sized banks precipitated a wave of suspensions. The panic failed to engulf the largest banks in all three cities. In Pittsburgh and Philadelphia, the largest and the strongest banks mobilized support for some of the troubled banks and thereby contributed to allaying the fear and uncertainty.

We have described the banking crises in each of the three cities as a mini panic since the brunt of the crisis was geographically constrained to certain parts of the city and mainly to specific bank classifications, namely savings banks including trust companies. Deposit losses amounted to no more than 8 percent of total bank deposits in each city.

What action, if any, was taken to moderate the mini panics once they were under way? The *Commercial and Financial Chronicle* (August 22, 1931, p. 1164) stated that there was no reason to think that the bank suspensions in Toledo in August 1931 were not strictly of local significance with little effect outside the area. But a similar statement might have been made about bank failures in Chicago, Pittsburgh, and Philadelphia. In at least one sense the bank closings were mainly local happenings. Bank suspensions in the four cities did not directly involve banks in other parts of the state or nation; that is, banks outside the four cities were not weakened directly by their failure.

But what we do not know and cannot demonstrate is how depositor confidence outside the four cities was adversely affected by events within those cities. Data on hoarding by Federal Reserve District do not enable us to locate precisely where the increased hoarding occurred. Conceivably, the increase in hoarding may have been concentrated in the city experiencing the bank suspensions; or it may have been diffused throughout the District. Friedman and Schwartz have maintained that failure of the Bank of United States in December 1930 affected depositor confidence nationwide, but they produced no evidence to support such a strong inference. Conceivably depositor confidence was affected adversely in the Boston Federal District between April and August 1931 by events outside the District since there were no failures within the District at that time. Hoarding in the New York District was too great to be explained by events within the District. And the hoarding that occurred represented outflows of currency to other Districts, not primarily increased holdings within the New York District.

What was the response to the mini panics in Philadelphia, Pittsburgh, and Chicago and the full scale panic in Toledo? Was the response mainly local as well? There is no evidence that the Federal Reserve Banks of Chicago, Cleveland, and Philadelphia took any positive action to intervene directly to keep open any of the troubled banks. No direct assistance was offered other than to discount eligible paper of the member banks. No accommodation was available to nonmember banks.

In both Philadelphia and Chicago leadership during the crisis was assumed by the leading bankers in the city with some support from the local Clearing House Association. In Philadelphia the role of both was minimal. The Clearing House ordered all banks to enforce the legal time delay of sixty days in the withdrawals of savings accounts. And on October 14 seven of the stronger banks announced that they would do whatever was necessary to prevent the Integrity Trust Company from failing, a bank with total deposits amounting to more than $60 million.

In Toledo attempts were made to merge the three banks that eventually failed, but those attempts were unsuccessful. The Federal Reserve Bank of Cleveland was prepared to offer assistance to the three remaining banks, but it did nothing as far as we know to prevent the earlier bank closings.

The banking crisis in Chicago in June 1930 evoked a response from the leaders of the largest banks in Chicago as well as the Clearing House Association that was in the best pre-Federal Reserve tradition. A merger was quickly arranged between the threatened Foreman State National Bank and the First National Bank of Chicago. The First National guaranteed unequivocally all the deposits of the Foreman banks, thereby thwarting a potentially dangerous bank run. And the Chicago Clearing House provided a guarantee of $10 million to indemnify First National against losses in liquidity of Foreman assets. Moreover, First National offered a full guarantee to the depositors of the Chicago Bank and Trust Company, a $17 million bank.

The hastily improvised leadership initiatives of the larger Chicago banks with the support of the Clearing House Association prevented the crisis from spreading to the Loop banks in the inner city. The bank failure rate and domestic hoarding decelerated. But there was no substantial increase in depositor confidence as reflected by a corresponding decrease in Federal Reserve notes in circulation.

4   The gold crisis: Britain's departure from the gold standard and the Fed's response

The reduction in the US monetary gold stock commenced immediately after Britain announced its departure from the gold standard – $114 million the first week and $156 million the second. This represented a dramatic change in gold movements compared with the first eight months of the year. Between January and June gold imports amounted to $363 million. Another $60 million was added between July and mid September. The magnitude of the outflow beginning in the final two weeks of September signalled the onset of a major redistribution of the world's gold stock between the US and the rest of the world, mainly France. Between September 25 and October 9, the Bank of France gained $1,193 million of gold. Some European central banks and private foreign banks were repatriating their gold balances in the US by the sale of bankers' acceptances for the purpose of strengthening their defense of gold convertibility and, in the case of France, to meet the hoarding demands of the public.

Table 3.4 shows the external and internal drains during the period of the crisis – September 23 to October 28. The external drain reached a peak in the week ending October 14 with an increase of more than $200 million. The drain subsided in the final two weeks of October. During this six-week period the monetary gold stock fell by $722 million, more than any other similar period in US history. At the same time hoarding

Table 3.4   *Changes in weekly monetary gold stock and currency in circulation, September 23 through October 28, 1931* ($m.)*

Date*	Change in monetary gold stock	Change in currency in circulation
September 23	−114	+76
September 30	−156	+82
October 7	−99	+185
October 14	−218	+42
October 21	−87	+32
October 28	−48	
	−722	+417

Note: * Wednesday figures.
Source: Board of Governors of the Federal Reserve System, *Banking and Monetary Statistics*, Washington DC, 1976, p. 386.

increased by $417 million, more than 80 percent of which occurred in the final two weeks of September and the first week of October. Both the external and the internal drains were substantial.

The relationship between the two drains is complex. Did the size of the external gold drain as well as Britain's departure from gold trigger a loss of confidence in the US banking system? I have no direct evidence that relates the increase in bank suspensions and hoarding to the external drain. But the effects of the gold drain on interest rates coupled with the Fed's delayed discount rate response may have weakened the public's perception of the soundness of the nation's banks and thus contributed to the increase in hoarding. The external drain may have created uncertainty about the future of gold convertibility, and thus general uncertainty was compounded when the public began to question the solvency of the banking system. Barrie Wigmore (1985, p. 219) thought that the British crisis had contributed to depositors' loss of confidence: "U.S. banks were thought to be exposed to heavy losses on their international loans and investments, although no reliable estimates were available on their magnitude." Furthermore, the collapse of the banking system in Germany and Austria "instilled in observers everywhere an awareness of the weakness of financial institutions which had appeared impregnable." Nevertheless, there is still no concrete evidence that ties specific bank suspensions to the gold drain. In fact in Pittsburgh it was the increase in bank failures that induced the increase in hoarding, not the external drain.

The significance of the gold drain cannot be discerned merely by its size alone. The monetary gold stock at the end of October 1931 was the same as it had been in January 1930. The gold reserve ratio – the ratio of gold held by the Fed to Federal Reserve notes and Deposit Liabilities – decreased from 78.4 percent on September 16 to 59.9 percent on October 28. Gold holdings in excess of legal reserve requirements amounted to $1.1 billion. A 40 percent legal reserve was required against Federal Reserve notes and 35 percent against deposit liabilities. Another $600 million of reserves could have been released if the $1 billion of gold certificates in circulation had been retired and Federal Reserve notes substituted. Federal Reserve notes required only a 40 percent backing. The amount of free gold, that is, gold held above all legal reserve requirements including gold used as collateral against Federal Reserve notes, was larger at the end of October than it had been when the gold drain began. The external drain never threatened the gold convertibility of the dollar. That does not mean, however, that the public and some foreign nationals did not perceive the gold drain as a distinct threat to gold convertibility in the US.

The effect of a $700 million plus reduction in the monetary gold stock, other things being equal, is an equivalent decrease in reserve deposits at the Federal Reserve. But reserve deposits did not decrease by anywhere near that amount. Other things did not remain equal. Currency in circulation (Federal Reserve notes plus Treasury currency) increased by approximately $400 million. The $1.1 billion decrease in reserve deposits was offset, though not completely, by a $961 million increase in bills bought and bills discounted. Reserve deposits decreased by $189 million as a result of gold sales and the increase in domestic hoarding. It is especially significant that these effects were achieved without open market operations. The monetary base actually increased by $200 million during the crisis period.

Table 3.5 shows changes in the determinants of reserve deposits between September 16 and October 28, 1931. The Federal Reserve was successful in preventing both the external and internal drains from having any negative effect on the monetary base. Fed officials intended to meet the internal drain by an increase in member bank indebtedness which we see from table 3.5 increased by $454 million, the external drain by an increase in the purchases of bankers' acceptances which increased by $507 million. Roy Young (1931), Governor of the Federal Reserve Bank of Boston and member of the Open Market Policy Conference, had told the Conference on August 11, 1931 that any emergency could be handled through the purchase of bills at a 1 percent rate. By continually making it attractive for banks to sell acceptances to the Fed, Reserve

Table 3.5 *Changes in determinants of reserve deposits, September 16–October 28, 1931*

Sources	Change ($m.)	Uses ($m.)	Change ($m.)
1 Bills discounted	+454	7 Currency in circulation	+393
2 Bills bought	+507	8 Treasury cash	+5
3 Government securities	−15	9 US Treasury deposits	+35
4 All other	−14	10 Nonmember deposits	−32
5 Monetary gold stock	−727	11 Other Federal Reserve assets	−6
6 Treasury currency outstanding	+1		
	+206		+395

Notes: * Wednesday figures.
Net change in reserve deposits −189.
Net change in monetary base +209.
Source: Board of Governors of the Federal Reserve System, *Banking and Monetary Statistics*, Washington DC, 1976, p. 386.

officials could inject reserves without all the publicity and fanfare of open market operations. The purchase of acceptances in lieu of government securities was a deliberately designed policy to minimize the impact of the gold drain on reserve deposits and the monetary base. The Fed's actions had the effect of minimizing changes in the monetary base during the gold crisis without resort to open market operations.

Preventing a decline in the monetary base, however, did not prevent the monetary aggregates from declining sharply. Between August and October demand deposits declined by over $1 billion and time deposits by $1.5 billion. M-1 fell by $719 million and M-2 by $2.2 billion. Since data are not available on M-1 and M-2 weekly, we include the entire month of September in our estimates.

The simple money multiplier model of Brunner and Meltzer $M = m *B$, where m is the M-1 or M-2 multiplier, depending upon the definition of M, and B is the monetary base, tells us that if the base remains unchanged to look for decreases in the multiplier as the source of the decline in M. The reserve–deposit ratio actually increased slightly, but the currency–deposit ratio increased by more than 10 percent.

Although the Fed was successful in preventing a decline in the monetary base, it made no effort to offset the effects on M of an increase in the currency–deposit ratio. The simple explanation for why the Fed failed to do so has been overlooked. Federal Reserve officials were very well aware of the existence of hoarding and the extent to which hoarding had proceeded in September and October. And they knew that an increase in hoarding would decrease reserve deposits, unless offset by bills purchased or open market operations. Why, then, did Reserve officials fail to monitor the currency–deposit ratio? There is a perfectly good reason.

Our understanding of the role of the currency–deposit ratio in the deposit expansion process was not articulated clearly before 1933 and 1934. Thomas Humphrey (1987) has traced the origins of the theory of the multiple expansion of deposits. He showed how the theory evolved with contributions of James Pennington, Robert Torrens, Alfred Marshall, and C.O. Phillips. But there was no recognition by any of these of the role of the currency–deposit ratio. Angell and Ficek in 1933 and James Meade in 1934 incorporated the currency–deposit ratio for the first time into a model of the deposit expansion process. Therefore, lack of knowledge, not ineptitude, played a paramount role in explaining why Fed officials did not respond to the increase in the currency–deposit ratio. They thought that it was sufficient to offset the effect of the internal drain on the monetary base, given existing knowledge of money stock determinants.

Bill buying and discount rate policy

As we have attempted to show, the Fed's bill buying policy coupled with liberal lending at the discount window was successful in offsetting most, if not all, the effects on reserve deposits generated by the external and internal drains. Although the Fed adjusted the bill buying rate upward in response to market-induced changes in the acceptance rate, the bill buying rate remained below the discount rate until October 16 when the two rates were equalized. The effect of the disparity between the two rates was to induce banks to sell acceptances to the Fed. This was a deliberate choice of instrument, not an accident of a passive adjustment to an unanticipated shock. The policy had been agreed to by the Directors of the New York Fed on September 10, eleven days before Britain announced its departure from gold. Governor Harrison (Discussion Notes 1931, p. 71), said that a firming of rates would not be undesirable, and that it should be the policy of the bank to permit seasonal demands for reserves during the autumn to be met passively by sales of acceptances to the Fed; that is, Fed officials expected tightening of the short-term money market. Bills bought increased by $487 million between September 23 and October 14 when there was a disparity between bill buying rate and the discount rate. After the two rates were equalized, the acquisition of bills decelerated.

The Fed's bill buying policy was an appropriate response to the external and internal drains when the objective was to prevent, if possible, the decline in reserve deposits. It is not the bill buying policy of the Fed that has been questioned but the absence of open market operations.

Two and a half weeks elapsed before Fed officials made the decision to raise the discount rate following Britain's departure from gold. Over $369 million of gold had either been exported or earmarked for export between September 21 and October 8 when the Federal Reserve Board approved unanimously the application of the Federal Reserve Bank of New York to increase the discount rate a full percentage point – from 1 1/2 to 2 1/2 percent. The Fed's decision was no "knee-jerk" response to gold standard conventions. The minutes of the September 24 meeting of the Directors of the New York Fed contain no record of discussions to raise the discount rate. A week later on October 1 Governor Harrison (Discussion Notes, October 1, 1931, p. 71) told the Directors that any rise in money rates would be regrettable for two reasons: (1) it might increase nervousness regarding the loss of gold; and (2) it might affect adversely the bond market. Furthermore, he explained that the Hoover administration was considering a proposal to establish a National Credit

Corporation to make advances to banks that no longer had a stock of eligible assets to discount at the Fed.

On the same day (October 1) C.S. Hamlin (1931, p. 148) and Adolph Miller, members of the Federal Reserve Board, recommended that New York increase the discount rate by half a percentage point immediately. They also considered the probable adverse effects on bond yields and concluded that it should be no obstacle to an increase in the discount rate. The Board and the New York Directors simply disagreed about the necessity for immediately raising the rate.

When New York requested approval for an increase on October 8, to be effective the next day, every member of the Board voted in favor. What happened, if anything, to change Harrison's mind about the desirability of a rate increase between October 1 and October 8? The gold outflow for the week ending October 7 was $50 million less than the preceding week. The internal drain, however, had increased by $100 million. We can only speculate about the policy switch. One consideration was Hoover's announcement on October 7 of a dramatic program for dealing with the financial crisis; that is, the creation of a voluntary credit pool for the explicit purpose of rediscounting the sound but frozen assets of banks in difficulty. Both Eugene Meyer, Governor of the Federal Reserve Board, and George Harrison were deeply involved in obtaining the cooperation of the New York bankers to participate in the new program. The discount rate increase may have been postponed until after Hoover's announcement on October 7, so as not to draw attention away from the President's initiatives.

A second consideration was Harrison's previous concerns about the effects of a rate increase on the gold outflow and the bond market may have evaporated. He (Discussion Notes, October 8, 1931, p. 85) told the New York Directors on October 8 that he doubted whether putting up the rate would either stop the gold outflow or reduce the internal drain! The effect of the increase on bond prices might be more than offset by the favorable effect of rate increases on bank earnings and thereby increase credit availability. In this way the increase in the discount rate would complement the president's proposal to restore bank solvency.

The third reason may have been that once Harrison realized how great the suspicion was abroad that the US might also devalue, he felt there was no other course open but to put up the discount rate.

The fourth reason for putting up the discount rate was purely technical, but no less persuasive for being so. Governor Harrison thought that it was appropriate to increase the discount rate in response to the prior changes in open market rates generated by gold exports and domestic hoarding so long as the increase did not have adverse effects on public psychology, by which he meant the desire to hoard currency at home and to ship gold abroad.

The conclusion to which we are inevitably drawn by the available evidence is that conventional gold standard considerations played a very minor role, if they played any role at all, in the decision of the New York Bank to advance the discount rate.

A week later on October 15 (effective October 16) the New York Bank requested and was granted permission to increase its rate another full percentage point to 3 1/2 percent. The outflow of gold had doubled in the week ending October 14 and hoarding had not declined. Harrison claimed once again that a technical basis still existed for an advance in its rate. Governor Meyer (Harrison Papers, Discussion Notes October 15, 1931, p. 92) of the Federal Reserve Board was present at the meeting of the New York Directors and said: "an advance in the rate was called for by every known rule, and believed that foreigners would regard it as a lack of courage if the rate were not advanced. ... he did not see how it would affect depositors." Board members in Washington were probably influenced more than the New York Directors by what was called for by adherence to the gold standard. The legacy of Governor Benjamin Strong to the New York Fed was a liberal interpretation of the so-called "rules." The New York Bank had never recognized any obligation to lower interest rates in response to substantial gold imports in 1922 out of concern for re-igniting inflation. Why, then, should the New York Bank officials automatically request an increase in the discount rate in response to a gold drain that did not impair gold convertibility of the dollar? The reasons why the Bank requested a rate increase in the first place, as I have attempted to show, were far more subtle than what is conveyed by the phrase in accordance with the "rules" of the gold standard game.

What were the effects of raising in two steps the discount rate from 1/2 to 3 1/2 percent? Friedman and Schwartz (1963, p. 317) were careful to point out that the increase in rates "was accompanied by a spectacular increase in bank failures and in runs on banks." To accompany does not imply to cause. And Friedman and Schwartz do not describe the mechanism or produce any telling evidence that causation necessarily went from the discount rate changes to accelerated bank suspensions. The discount rate increase could conceivably have been an unanticipated shock imparting uncertainty about the solvency of the banking system. But it is also equally plausible that the initial shock was not the discount rate increase but the uncertainty generated by Britain's departure from gold. The bank failure rate had accelerated in the two and a half weeks *before* the discount rate was advanced.

The first part of this chapter assigned a significant role to the mini panics in Pittsburgh, Philadelphia, and Chicago in explaining the September–October banking crisis. The full impact of bank suspensions in these three cities was felt *before* October 9 when New York put up the discount rate to 2 1/2 percent. Between October 2 and October 9 sixteen Philadelphia banks failed with unrevised deposit losses totalling $70 million. Sixteen banks failed in Pittsburgh and contiguous counties between September 21 and October 1 with deposit losses of $73 million. Chicago had nine bank suspensions between September 20 and October 9 with estimated deposit losses of $22 million. Combined bank suspensions and deposit losses in the three cities for the period September 20 to October 9 were forty-one and $165 million respectively. Putting up the discount rate, therefore, played no causal role in explaining bank suspensions, deposit losses, and domestic hoarding during the first three weeks of the banking crisis. Nor does the hoarding evidence support the view that putting up the discount rate initiated the banking panic. Federal Reserve notes in circulation increased by $439 million between September 16 and November 4 (see appendix 3.2). Fully 60 percent of the increase in domestic hoarding took place between September 16 and October 7 before the New York Bank raised its discount rate. The discount rate increase, therefore, could have accounted, at most, for 40 percent of the increase in hoarding. That is not to deny that the Fed's rate response may have played a contributing role in the fourth and fifth weeks of the crisis.

The rise in short-term rates was relatively moderate and short lived. Prime commercial paper rose 200 basis points; prime bankers' acceptances had risen 236 basis points since September 21. The average rate on new Treasury issues increased from 1.21 percent in September to 2.47 percent in October. The yield spread widened for low-grade relative to high-grade securities. It was the 10 percent or more decline in certain long-term securities prices that may have affected the solvency of many banks and accelerated the bank failure rate. But it does not follow that the increases in the discount rate caused the bond depreciation. Bond depreciation may equally have been due to security fire-sales by troubled banks suffering large deposit withdrawals.

It is not possible to conclude from the available evidence what effects the increase in the discount rate had on domestic hoarding and the bank failure rate as distinguished from the effects associated with the gold outflow. The evidence from the timing would suggest that substantial hoarding and increases in bank suspensions had occurred *before* the Fed raised the discount rate. The increase in the rate may have exacerbated hoarding and bank suspensions but did not cause the initial increase.

National Credit Corporation

On October 7 two days before the increase in the discount rate, President Hoover with great fanfare announced a program to restore confidence in the banking system. He had become convinced that the Fed on its own initiative could not, or would not, take the requisite action to stabilize the banking situation. The financial turmoil in Western Europe in July had created an atmosphere of caution and fear at home resulting in increased bank failures and accelerated hoarding in August and September. The Fed, he believed, was helpless in not being able to assist thousands of solvent, nonmember banks, and that the amount of eligible paper held by weaker but solvent member banks was not adequate to meet their liquidity needs. It was imperative that some action should be taken to relieve the banking situation. A mechanism, he thought, must be found to increase liquidity by reducing the pressure on security markets generated by fire-sales by the troubled banks. They then might be more willing to increase credit availability and thereby stimulate economic activity.

Hoover planned to create a $500 million credit pool through a voluntary association of bankers for the explicit purpose of rediscounting the sound but frozen assets of banks in difficulty. In effect, the larger more liquid banks would redistribute their funds to smaller and weaker banks. On October 13 a National Credit Corporation was formally organized with member banks required to contribute 2 percent of their net time and demand deposits to be eligible to receive assistance. Local committees of bankers would receive applications for loans and allocate funds, the main criterion for aid being the solvency of the individual bank.

The Corporation was to begin work immediately. However, by December only $10 million of loans had been made. Both bank suspensions and hoarding had begun to subside at the end of October. For the week ending October 7, hoarding had increased by more than $100 million. The week following Hoover's announcement, the increase was reduced by two-thirds. Officials of the National Credit Corporation decided to suspend making loans in November.

Hoover's plan to create a voluntary credit pool did not originate with Britain's departure from gold. He first broached the idea of voluntary cooperative action by the bankers themselves in a meeting with Eugene Meyer, Governor of Federal Reserve Board, on September 8. Britain abandoned gold on September 21. Three weeks elapsed before Meyer could arrange a meeting with New York bankers in Washington. To insure absolute secrecy, the meeting took place at Andrew Mellon's (Secretary of the Treasury) apartment in Washington on October 4 when the bankers agreed to organize a voluntary association provided that Hoover would agree to establish a government corporation in the event the National Credit Corporation failed to achieve its goal.

The amount of dollar assistance made available in October was minuscule and could not by itself have contributed to alleviating the crisis generated when Britain abandoned gold. Nevertheless, the announcement effects may have played a significant role in reducing the number of bank failures and the amount of hoarding in the weeks that followed. The view that Hoover's action may have alleviated the banking crisis is supported by the *New York Times* (November 9 and December 19, 1931) who claimed that the number of bank failures dropped weekly after the Hoover announcement. But that claim is difficult to verify since there are no official data on bank failures weekly. George Harrison testified that the National Credit Corporation could not be judged solely by the amount of money loaned. He thought that the main effect of Hoover's proposal was psychological; it tended to restore confidence of both the bankers and the depositors. Harrison (Hearings 1932, p. 68) stated that there was an "unholy fear" on the part of many bankers that deposit withdrawals would continue unabated. To him it was no mere coincidence that immediately following Hoover's public statement, the rate of bank failures declined as well as deposit withdrawals:

As figures which you have available will show, the outstanding currency in the country, has declined now well below what it was at the peak; and while there was some increase after the creation of the corporation; the rate of increase was most substantially checked immediately after it was announced.

More to the point:

We have contacts, of course, with the banks throughout our district – very close and very intimate. The whole psychology of the bankers' mind – especially the smaller country banker, who did not have a very good contact – was immediately changed.

Ogden Mills (Hearings, 1932, p. 54), Undersecretary of the Treasury, also testified reaffirming much of what Harrison had said about the decrease in bank failures and hoarding. He also felt that the effects of Hoover's announcement were largely psychological:

I feel very strongly that the setting up of that organization at the time it was set up these banks had a very great influence, if not a preponderating influence, in restoring stability to the credit situation in October. The mere existence of the fund, the mere evidence of the fact that the banking community of the United States stood ready to act with solidarity ... restored confidence, the evidence of which was immediately obvious both at home and abroad.

Anecdotal evidence leaves much to be desired. Nevertheless, we have no really equally attractive alternative hypothesis about what brought the September–October crisis to a halt; that is, why the crisis reached its zenith in the second week of October and diminished in intensity thereafter. The increase in the discount rate may have been a determining consideration as well.

The Hoover proposal, however, may have exacerbated the gold outflow during the week ending October 14. The outflow was twice that of the preceding week and fell by one-half in the succeeding week. Dispatches from the *New York Times* (October 9, 1931) correspondents described the mood in Paris as despondent: "the Paris Press shows a tendency to regard the moves in the United States as toward inflation and a weakening of American credit."
And again on October 11:

French public is being led to believe that the United States is going in for a wholesale inflation, and that in such inflation there is immense danger to the dollar ... panic is being spread more and more extensively, just as was done weeks ago with regard to sterling.

Two Bank of France officials were sent immediately to the US to find out how Hoover's program was supposed to deal with banking conditions in the US. A French delegation led by Prime Minister Laval came to the US in October, according to Eichengreen (1992, p. 294) "to hammer out conditions for maintaining the dollar deposits of the Bank of France."

French fears were allayed and together with Hoover's announcement of new initiatives to deal with the banking crisis, hoarding, bank failures, and gold exports eventually subsided. The crisis was over by the end of the month.

5   Was there something special about the 1931 banking crisis?

Did the 1931 banking crisis differ from other banking crises in US history? The September–October crisis is distinctive in several important ways. The leveling off in the number of bank suspensions, deposits in failed banks and hoarding at the end of October did not lead to a return flow of currency to the banking system. Confidence in the solvency of the banks was not restored; the erosion of confidence was only temporarily abated. Additional evidence that the amount of hoarded currency did not abate when the panic ended is the behavior of large denominational currency (Federal Reserve notes of $50 and above). The amount of large denominational currency never fell below its December 1931 amount throughout 1932. This behavior contrasts sharply with the banking panic in January–March 1933. Currency in circulation increased by $1.9 billion between February 21 and March 8. The ending of the panic was followed during the next three weeks by a massive return flow of currency to the banks of $1.2 billion symptomatic of the decrease in bank suspensions and a restoration of confidence. By the end of July 1933 there had been a further reduction of currency in circulation of $700 million. Large denominational currency fell continuously by $418 million between March and October 1933. There was no similar return flow in November and December 1931.

The banking situation at the end of October had been stabilized temporarily at a very low level of depositor confidence in the banks. With confidence levels so depressed, depositors were hypersensitive to additional shocks that would simply trigger a renewal of bank suspensions. The banking panic of September–October, therefore, did not end in October, if by ending we mean a restoration of confidence, nor did it end in December.

What is distinctive about the 1931 crisis by contrast with pre-1914 banking panics, is that it did not have its origin in the central money market. The initial impact of the September–October crisis was felt first in Pittsburgh then Philadelphia, and Chicago. Hoarding in New York City increased significantly but that was not the consequence of a wave of bank failures in the New York District. Demands for currency by foreign nationals and banks in the interior were centered in New York.

There is no discernible pattern in the diffusion of the crisis from certain regional centers to the periphery. One reason for the absence of such a pattern is the fact that the panic did not at any time engulf any of the largest banks of Philadelphia, Pittsburgh, and Chicago. Exactly how the loss of confidence spread across the twelve Federal Reserve Districts is still a matter requiring an explanation. It is not very enlightening to say that a contagion of fear swept over the country with a differential impact by District. Even if we cannot explain how fear was diffused, we can measure its magnitude by weekly changes in Federal Reserve notes in circulation in individual Districts. And that is what we have attempted to do. Moreover, we can identify the shock or shocks that generated fear and uncertainty such as Britain's departure from gold and the Fed's increase in the discount rate.

It is also important to bear in mind that there was a significant regime change with the establishment of the Federal Reserve System. In pre-1914 bank panics, remedies included suspension of convertibility of deposits into currency and frequently the issue of Clearing House Certificates. After 1914 the Fed supposedly was the sole source of supplying liquidity when banks were threatened by the loss of depositor confidence. We have seen, however, how Philadelphia banks banded together to guarantee the solvency of some banks in difficulty, a pre-1914 remedy.

We have been able to account for a sizeable proportion of deposits in suspended banks and domestic hoarding by looking closely at bank failures in three cities, Pittsburgh, Philadelphia, and Chicago. And it is clear that the source of the bank closings in each of these cities was runs on banks. Panic did motivate some depositors, especially those of trust companies in Pittsburgh and Philadelphia in the last week of September and the first two weeks of October. But in neither place did the press describe these bank suspensions as a panic gripping all of the city's depositors. The loss of confidence was confined to a particular class of banks and usually those located on the periphery rather than in the central city.

So far we have not been able to find any direct link to the disturbances in the three cities to increased suspensions in contiguous areas, for example, the effect of bank suspensions in Chicago and the suspension rate in the Minneapolis District.

Our analysis would tend to suggest that the waves of bank suspensions in September–October do not appear to have conformed fully to the conventional view of a banking panic; that is, there was no *indiscriminate* run on banks by depositors whose confidence in banking institutions in a given area had been shattered. Bank runs, especially among urban banks, appear to have been directed against particular banks that were known to be weak. The historian of Chicago banking Cyril James (1938, p. 1034), for example, concluded that prior to June 1932 bank runs in the city were "directed against particular banks that were known to be enfeebled", whereas the bank run in June 1932 "was directed against the whole Chicago money market." We have attempted to show how bank runs in Pittsburgh and Philadelphia were limited to particular sections of the city and to certain savings banks and trust companies. There was no indiscriminate run on larger banks at the city's financial center. I have attempted to capture the distinction between what happened, or what was supposed to happen, in a classic banking panic and what actually happened in Chicago, Pittsburgh, and Philadelphia by labelling banking unrest in these three cities "mini panics."

6   Role of the 1931 banking crises in contributing to the Great Depression

Finally we may ask: what role did the region specific (April–August) and the nationwide (September–October) banking crises play during the

Great Depression? Friedman and Schwartz (1963) attributed a causal role to bank failures during the first banking crisis in 1930. They maintained that an autonomous disturbance in the currency–deposit ratio provoked a rash of bank suspensions leading to a contraction of the money stock and eventually to a decline in output and employment, though they left vague one of the sources of the disturbance that forced a revision of depositors' expectations of future losses. Peter Temin (1976) denied the causal link between bank suspensions and output. He conjectured, and it was only a conjecture, that a decline in lower-grade bond prices induced by a decline in income was the source of bank failures; that is, the relationship between bank failures and income was endogenous.

Apparently Friedman and Schwartz (1963, p. 313) assigned a causal role to the banking crisis of 1931 as well although there is no explicit statement to that effect. The implication is strong in the following statement:

In March, a second banking crisis started a renewed decline in the stock of money and at an accelerated rate. A month or two later, a renewed decline started in economic activity in general, and the hope of revival that season was ended.

But they also recognized that runs on banks led to fire-sales of securities, a depression of security prices, and ultimately to banking suspensions. And they concluded:

The impairment in the market value of assets held by banks, particularly in their bond portfolios, was the most important source of impairment of capital leading to bank suspensions, rather than the default of specific loans or of specific bond issues. (p. 355)

A similar diagnosis was presented to the Open Market Policy Conference on October 26 (Executive Committee Minutes, October 26, 1931). The Committee was told that depreciation in the market value of bond holdings was probably responsible for the difficulties of more banks than any other single cause. Between September 16 and October 19 the market value of US government securities declined by 8 percent, low grade bonds even more.

Temin (1976, p. 84) in a summary of prevailing opinion stated that "The principal reason usually given for subsequent bank failures [after 1930] is the decline in the capital value of bank portfolios coming from the decline in the market value of securities." For a position presumably so widely held, there is a surprising deficiency of evidence, and what hard evidence there is seems to point in the opposite direction!

A special Committee was appointed by the Federal Reserve Board in

1930 to study bank suspensions in the US during the period 1921–31. The Committee's report was never published. Volume V is entitled *Bank Suspensions in the United States, 1892–1931*. Part of the Committee's task was to analyze carefully bank suspensions in 1931. A sample of 105 member banks from the twelve Federal Reserve Districts that closed in 1931 was selected to represent the size and geographical distribution of the suspended banks. Much of the information was taken from bank examiners' reports with data obtained on bond and security holdings of only those banks that closed in 1931. Nearly one-third of the sampled banks were criticized by bank examiners for the quality of their investments. Bond depreciation, however, was the primary cause of failures in *only* six of the 105 and an important contributory cause in four others, that is, less than 10 percent. Moreover, a study of the bond accounts revealed that the bond portfolios in farming communities were of a higher grade than banks in cities for at least two reasons: the bond account was a smaller percentage of deposits, and banks were required to hold high-grade municipal and other securities against their US government deposits. Garlock and Gile's (1935, p. 35) study of bank failures in Arkansas revealed that the depreciation of securities was not a major cause of bank suspensions in Arkansas before the end of 1932. Although it is much too early to render any final verdict on the causes of the bank suspensions in 1931, the available evidence as sparse as it might be does not support the Friedman, Schwartz, and Temin conjectures about the causal role of the depreciation in bank prices and bank suspensions.

The simultaneous occurrence of accelerated bank suspensions and Britain's departure from the gold standard suggests another plausible explanation for bank closings. The abandonment of gold was the exogenous shock that led to a revision of depositor expectations of future losses. And expectations of increased depositor losses increased hoarding which triggered bank suspensions. Unfortunately, the microhistorical account fails to confirm this conjecture. There is nothing specific that ties the bank suspensions, for example, in Pittsburgh, Philadelphia, and Chicago to the gold crisis. I have not been able to identify a single bank suspension, large or small, that can be traced directly to events connected with Britain's departure from gold. Why depositors in the interior of the country should have been expected to have reacted differently from depositors in New York City banks with some foreign securities exposure is puzzling to consider. That is not to deny that such a relationship existed only that the channels through which depositor confidence was adversely affected by events in Europe are exceptionally difficult to identify. I have simply not been successful in uncovering what the channels of influence were, if any.

Another important cause of bank suspensions, though it would be difficult to say how important, was deposit "seepage," a term employed at the time to mean long-term continuous declines in deposits not motivated primarily by a contagion of fear. In those agricultural regions where farm income fell more rapidly than farm outlay, we might reasonably expect unfavorable local and regional trade balances. Deposit losses led to reserve losses followed by a subsequent contraction of loans and investments. Data on bank deposits show a general movement of funds from agricultural to financial and industrial centers during the Great Depression. Two pieces of evidence tend to support this assertion: (1) The ratio of nonmember bank total deposits to total deposits of all commercial banks declined from 24.5 percent on December 21, 1929 to 20.2 percent on December 31, 1932; it fell to 16.8 percent one year later. (2) The ratio of total deposits of 101 weekly reporting member banks to total deposits of all commercial banks increased from 47.3 percent in 1929 to 58.7 percent in 1932. A peak was reached of 60.9 percent in 1933. Both of these indicators are imprecise and do not measure exactly the deposit redistribution from rural agricultural areas to industrial and financial centers. All nonmember banks are not located in agricultural areas, but the vast majority are. The direction of the trend, however, is reliably represented. A geographical redistribution of deposits should not affect the overall level of deposits. A rural deficit should be offset by an urban surplus. Nevertheless, the outflow of deposits from rural banks, if persistent and continuous, would increase their vulnerability to failure.

7   Summary and conclusions

The purpose of this chapter has been to reconstruct the nationwide banking panic following Britain's departure from gold convertibility on September 21 and continuing through October 31, 1931. Reconstructing the crisis entailed identifying the number of bank suspensions and deposits of suspended banks geographically; that is, by Federal Reserve District, and, whenever possible, by specific city or rural area. Equally, if not more important, was to measure the loss of depositor confidence in the banking system. We employed as an index of depositor confidence weekly data by Reserve District on Federal Reserve notes in circulation (hoarding). The last, and the far more difficult task, was to attempt to classify bank suspensions attributable to bank runs and to voluntary and involuntary closings because of deposit "seepage" and deterioration of net worth occurring over an extended period of time. No official data exists with which to make such a classification.

We have, I believe, been partially successful in having been able to identify the three US cities where mini panics occurred, that is, bank runs that were largely confined to smaller banks and trust companies and one city, Toledo, with a full-scale panic. Deposit losses of suspended banks and increases in domestic hoarding were highly concentrated, as we attempted to show, in three Federal Reserve Districts: Cleveland, Philadelphia, and Chicago.

The September–October banking crisis did not have its origin in the New York money market; there was no crisis in the central money market. Bank suspensions were negligible and the runup of short-term interest rates was moderate. Some European central banks and private foreign banks were repatriating their deposit balances for gold. Likewise, they were selling acceptances for the purpose of using the proceeds to export or earmark for export gold. Furthermore, the collapse of the banking systems in Austria and Germany during the summer imparted an awareness of the vulnerability of the US banking system as well, especially to the increased risk of loss on their international loans and investments. Uncertainty about the future of gold convertibility may also have contributed to the loss of depositor confidence.

There is, however, no direct link between the gold crisis and the mini panics in Pittsburgh and Philadelphia in late September and early October. We have concluded from the evidence from the hoarding data that the loss of depositor confidence was widely, though unequally, diffused across the country.

We have demonstrated that there was no nationwide banking crisis between April and August though there were significant increases in the number of bank suspensions, deposits in closed banks, and domestic hoarding. The April–August disturbance was region specific with Chicago and the contiguous area being the center. The gold crisis precipitated by Britain's departure from gold turned what had been a region-specific banking disturbance into a full-fledged nationwide banking panic.

The Fed's response was not a knee-jerk reaction prompted by purely conventional gold standard considerations. The New York bank had learned in the 1920s not to react automatically to inflows of gold that jeopardized price stability. Why, then, should they react to gold outflows without regard to the economic consequences of their actions? The New York Fed delayed increasing the discount rate for almost three weeks, half-way through the September–October banking panic. By that time the banking panic was fully underway. The increase in the discount rate on October 9 could not have played a causal role in initiating the crisis, though it may have been a contributing factor during the last two weeks of the crisis. Moreover, the Fed's failure to offset the depressing effects of increases in the currency–deposit ratio on the money stock cannot be labelled inept since knowledge of how the currency–deposit ratio affected the money stock was not forthcoming until 1933 and 1934.

Reserve officials understood that an increase in gold exports and domestic hoarding would tend to reduce reserve deposits, and they fully employed the bill-buying and borrowing instruments to neutralize their effects. The monetary base increased during the banking crisis. Their response was in accordance with the knowledge available at that time. It would be anachronistic to attribute knowledge of the money stock process to Reserve officials in 1931 that was only available after 1933.

President Hoover took the initiative in early October to end the banking crisis. Not because of the Fed's ineptness and reluctance to act but because he thought that the Fed did not have the power to assist nonmember banks, and the weaker member banks did not have adequate eligible paper to meet their liquidity needs at the discount window. The effectiveness of the National Credit Corporation did not reside in the amount of assistance rendered but in the boost it gave to depositor confidence and thereby shortening the duration of the banking crisis.

Table A3.1 *Federal Reserve notes in circulation monthly by Federal Reserve District, 1931** *($m.)*

	Boston	New York	Philadelphia	Cleveland	Richmond	Atlanta	Chicago	St. Louis	Minneapolis	Kansas City	Dallas	San Francisco	TOTAL
January 31	127	289	139	179	86	133	143	80	49	66	28	160	1,479
February 25	125	257	140	182	82	129	150	78	48	66	26	166	1,449
March 25	132	246	137	178	79	130	165	76	48	65	27	158	1,441
April 29	136	269	135	184	76	130	222	75	47	64	27	161	1,526
May 27	136	273	147	192	73	127	230	73	47	63	27	164	1,552
June 24	133	279	144	198	71	121	349	72	49	63	27	168	1,674
July 29	136	305	146	199	67	115	382	72	49	63	27	176	1,737
August 26	139	398	149	240	67	113	417	73	51	68	27	203	1,945
September 30	143	406	172	264	82	112	456	77	57	70	36	223	2,098
October 28	148	498	271	311	99	120	491	86	63	79	51	230	2,449
November 26	148	499	274	312	99	119	493	85	64	81	50	227	2,451
December 31	195	563	272	321	106	120	519	87	69	83	47	230	2,612

Note: * Wednesday figures.
Source: Commercial and Financial Chronicle, 1931.

Table A3.2 *Federal Reserve notes in circulation weekly in each of twelve Federal Reserve Districts, September 16–November 4, 1931 ($m.)*

Federal Reserve District	September 16	September 23	September 30	October 7	October 14	October 21	October 28	November 4
Boston	138	142	143	145	153	156	148	148
New York	388	389	406	447	456	467	471	498
Philadelphia	162	167	172	220	233	261	262	271
Cleveland	243	250	264	279	286	296	304	311
Richmond	73	80	82	88	92	98	97	99
Atlanta	112	112	112	115	117	118	118	120
Chicago	447	453	456	484	487	488	484	491
St. Louis	76	76	77	78	80	83	85	85
Minneapolis	55	56	57	61	61	62	62	63
Kansas City	69	70	70	72	75	76	76	79
Dallas	30	31	36	51	52	50	51	51
San Francisco	214	219	223	230	229	228	226	230
TOTAL	2,007	2,045	2,098	2,270	2,321	2,383	2,384	2,446

Source: Commercial and Financial Chronicle, 1931.

Table A3.3   *Number of bank suspensions, and deposits in failed banks by Federal Reserve District monthly, 1931*

Federal Reserve District	January		February		March		April		May		June	
	No.	$m.	No.	$m.	No.	$m.	No.	$m.	No.	$m.	No.	$m.
Boston	0	0	0	0	1	2.3	0	0	0	0	0	0
New York	2	6.3	0	0	3	3.1	4	4	0	0	4	13.6
Philadelphia	3	1.6	4	3.3	2	1.7	3	2.1	7	6.8	5	2
Cleveland	6	3.2	16	8.4	7	1.4	6	7.2	7	4.2	10	23.3
Richmond	18	5.2	2	0.6	5	2	7	3.9	7	0.2	9	3.3
Atlanta	37	22	10	0.1	6	0.6	3	4.9	4	0.4	4	1.8
Chicago	49	16.6	12	10.7	40	19.1	17	10.2	25	15.5	80	137
St. Louis	40	13.8	15	2.2	9	0	2	0	6	1.0	5	1.3
Minneapolis	13	3.1	3	3.5	8	2.9	11	1.7	13	3.7	31	7.4
Kansas City	16	1.7	7	1.6	4	0.9	5	0.3	9	3	11	1.9
Dallas	4	0.6	4	2.2	3	1.3	2	0.6	4	0.5	5	1.7
San Francisco	0	0.9	5	1.1	1	0	3	1.2	5	0.4	3	0.6
Total	188	75	78	34	89	35	63	36	87	36	167	194
Rev.	198	76	76	35	86	34	64	42	91	43	167	190

July		August		September		October		November		December			
No.	$m.	No.	$m.	No.	$m.	No.	$m.	No.	$m.	No.	$m.	No.	$m.
0	0	0	0	1	0.2	5	24.2	0	0	26	100	33	126.5
2	2.8	13	50.6	7	8.6	11	28.2	6	3.2	28	40.3	80	160.7
2	1.3	1	1	12	22	47	96	4	3.1	8	8.9	98	149.8
9	3.4	23	96.2	23	56.6	49	177.8	9	10.4	17	23	182	415
4	0.1	7	1	25	33.5	64	33.6	11	8	38	31.2	197	122.6
1	0.4	2	0.7	13	1.5	20	5.3	20	7.9	13	7.1	133	53.3
29	11.7	43	17.8	97	53.4	107	91.1	33	10.2	93	52.5	625	429.7
3	0	10	1.1	29	6.3	53	23.5	29	7.2	54	14.9	255	71.3
23	4.5	28	3.2	51	15.4	53	10	19	2.7	19	4.4	272	62.5
11	1.9	20	9.6	19	3.1	62	15.5	28	5.3	30	6.4	222	51.2
5	1.9	3	1.7	14	23.6	33	14.3	10	4	6	1.2	93	53.6
									1.7				
3	0	4	20.2	12	1	10	2.6	6	88	21	19.5	73	49.2
92	28	154	203.1	303	203	514	522	175	68	353	310		1,787
93	41	158	180	305	234	522	471	175		358	277	2,293	1,691

Source: Author's estimates.

4 The banking panic of 1933

The banking panic of 1933 is an anomaly among US financial panics. In no other financial panic was there such widespread use of bank moratoria or bank holidays for forestalling bank suspensions. In no other financial panic did the initiative for closing the banks or restricting deposit withdrawals reside with officials of the individual states. A bank moratorium or banking holiday was a legal artifice for closing a bank or banks temporarily without jeopardizing their solvency. The suspension of cash payment had been a characteristic feature of pre-1914 panics, but the decision to suspend payment had been made by individual banks in smaller towns and Clearing House Associations in the larger cities. The use of statewide moratoria was not new; five states had declared banking holidays in 1907. However, at no time had bank moratoria been used more extensively than in the three weeks following the declaration of the Michigan banking holiday on February 14, 1933. By the end of the day on March 4, banks had been closed in thirty-three states; deposit restrictions were in effect in ten, and optional closing in five. In no other panic had banking operations been curtailed so drastically.

Bank moratoria introduced a new source of depositor uncertainty. In the conventional panic depositor uncertainty had its origin in the questionable solvency of more than one bank. Bank moratoria created additional uncertainty among depositors about when and if state banking officials would close all the banks in a particular state. Moreover, the restrictions on deposit withdrawals increased the demands for currency. The bank holiday was the mechanism for transmitting banking unrest from state to state. The declaration of a banking holiday in one state motivated depositors to withdraw deposits from out-of-state banks to meet their immediate transactions needs thereby transmitting withdrawal pressures to contiguous states and to the New York and Chicago money markets. Moreover, depositors in surrounding states became alarmed that similar deposit restrictions would be imposed in their states and would therefore rush to withdraw deposits in anticipation of a bank moratorium. In an attempt to protect the interest of small depositors and to forestall further bank suspensions, state officials responded by the declaration of banking holidays without apparently any regard to what effect their behavior might have on other states and the rest of the country. A sequence of uncoordinated bank moratoria describes how the panic was disseminated throughout the country.

Why indeed did it become necessary to resort to a pre-1914 recipe for coping with the 1933 banking panic? Had not the Federal Reserve System been established to make the suspension of cash payments obsolete? Suspension of cash payments had been avoided in the three previous banking crises of the Great Depression. What explains its revival in February and March 1933?

Before the creation of the National Credit Corporation by President Hoover in the midst of the third banking crisis in October 1931, there was no legislative authority for assisting distressed banks unless a national banking panic threatened. Lender-of-last-resort responsibilities of the Fed applied solely to panic-generated distress and, narrowly interpreted, to banks that were members of the Federal Reserve System. The acceleration of both panic and nonpanic-related bank suspensions in 1931 led President Hoover to propose the establishment of a National Credit Corporation, an agency whose purpose it would be to lend to solvent but illiquid member banks with an inadequate supply of eligible paper to discount at the Fed. In early 1932 the agency was transformed into the Reconstruction Finance Corporation (RFC) and was empowered to lend to all banks in need.

Making provision for aiding distressed banks through the RFC necessarily blurred the lender-of-last-resort responsibilities of the Fed. By what criteria can we segregate those banks whose distress could precipitate a panic and those that could not? Would the Fed be responsible for the former, and the RFC the latter? What inevitably contributed to the confusion about responsibility was the appointment of Eugene Meyer, Governor of the Federal Reserve Board, to serve also as Chairman of the RFC!

During the three week crisis in late February and early March the RFC played a key role in attempting to find a solution to the Michigan banking crisis but without success. And the initiatives of Hoover and the Federal Reserve were likewise rejected leaving state banking officials no other option but to close the banks. No one regarded a bank moratorium as a solution; it was merely a stopgap measure to forestall bank insolvencies while a permanent remedy could be forged. A sequence of bank moratoria followed the closing of the Michigan banks culminating in the declaration of a national banking holiday by President Roosevelt on March 6. Wigmore (1985) and Donaldson (1992) have maintained that external, not internal, considerations were primarily responsible for Roosevelt's action. They considered the gold reserve position of the New York Fed as paramount, not the collapsed state of the banking industry. The evidence suggests that both considerations were decisive. The panic ended when the government assumed responsibility for reopening the closed banks as mandated by the Emergency Banking Act of 1933.

The first section summarizes briefly the banking situation in 1932. The second describes what happened during the three-week period prior to the declaration of a national banking holiday. The third examines the external gold drain; the fourth sets out what happened in the money and the capital markets during the panic; the fifth describes the response of the Federal Reserve to the impending crisis; the sixth looks at the expenditure effects of the crisis; the seventh examines the resolution of the crisis; and the final section draws some conclusions from the preceding analysis.

1   The long pause between financial storms: 1932

The banking situation in the US improved in 1932, but there was little cause to rejoice. The number of bank suspensions had declined from a high in 1931 of 2,293 to 1,453 in 1932, a decline of 37 percent. Nevertheless, bank failures remained a serious problem. Some semblance of national banking stability returned in February following almost continuous panic-like disturbances between April and October 1931. Contributing to the improved banking scene were numerous loans made by the newly created Reconstruction Finance Corporation (January, 1931) to troubled banks. By July the RFC had made $643 million in loans to 3,600 banks. Furthermore, the Open Market Policy Conference had undertaken the purchase of $1 billion of government securities, $25 million a week at first and $100 million a week thereafter. Hoarding as measured by either currency in circulation or currency outside banks seasonally adjusted declined continuously through May. There was an uptick in June and July after which the decline resumed; currency in circulation ended the year at levels slightly less than at the beginning. Depositor confidence had not eroded further in 1932, a positive step at least in the right direction.

Table 4.1 shows the number of bank suspensions, deposits in failed banks, and currency in circulation monthly for 1932. What is most striking is the marked increase in all three indicators in June and July reminiscent of previous banking crises in 1930 and 1931. A comparison with other banking crises of the Great Depression is provided in table 4.2.

Table 4.1   *Number of bank suspensions, deposits in failed banks, and currency in circulation monthly, 1932*

Month	Number of bank suspensions	Deposits in failed banks ($m.)	Currency held by public* ($m.)	Currency in circulation* ($m.)
January	342	219	4,896	5,375
February	119	52	4,824	5,400
March	45	11	4,743	5,285
April	74	32	4,751	5,220
May	82	34	4,746	5,225
June	151	133	4,959	5,305
July	132	49	5,048	5,510
August	85	30	4,988	5,475
September	67	14	4,941	5,375
October	102	20	4,863	5,295
November	93	43	4,842	5,265
December	161	71	4,830	5,210
Total	1,453	708		

Note: * Seasonally adjusted.
Source: Bank Suspensions and Deposits in Failed Banks: Board of Governors of the Federal Reserve System, *Federal Reserve Bulletin*, September 1937, p. 907. Currency Held by the Public: Milton Friedman and Anna Schwartz, *Monetary History of the United States*, Princeton, 1963, p. 713. Currency in Circulation: Board of Governors of the Federal Reserve System, *Banking and Monetary Statistics 1914–1941*, Washington, DC 1976, p. 414.

Table 4.2   *Number of bank suspensions, deposits in failed banks, and currency in circulation seasonally adjusted during the 1930 and 1931 crises and June–July 1932*

Banking crises	Number of suspensions	Deposits in failed banks ($m.)	Currency in circulation seasonally adjusted
Nov. 1930–Jan. 1931	806	628	270
April–August 1931	573	496	350
Sept.–Oct. 1932	827	705	425
June–July 1932	283	182	285

Source: See tables 2.1, 3.1, and 4.1.

Friedman and Schwartz did not identify the June–July episode as one of the banking crises of the Great Depression. No mention is even made of it! It is clear that the banking disturbance in June and July does not compare in severity with the earlier crises if we look solely at the number of bank suspensions and deposits in failed banks. Both bank closings and deposits in suspended banks are much smaller. However, if we look a little closer we see that the increase in currency in circulation in June and July 1932 was slightly higher than it had been during the first banking crisis in 1930. Judged solely by the loss of depositor confidence as proxied by currency in circulation, the two episodes are remarkably similar. The one has as much right to be treated as a banking crisis or panic as the other. We concluded earlier that the first and second banking crises were region specific. As we shall see, the June–July crisis was region specific but confined largely to the city of Chicago and the contiguous area. Approximately one-half of the suspended banks and deposits in failed banks in June and July were located in the Chicago Federal Reserve District. Federal Reserve notes in circulation increased $305 million between June 8 and July 21. Of that amount the Chicago District accounted for more than 60 percent of the increase. The concentration of hoarding in the Chicago District is revealed in table 4.3 which shows the change in Federal Reserve notes in circulation by Federal Reserve District between June 8 and July 21.

It is clear from table 4.4 that bank suspensions in the city of Chicago began to accelerate in the middle of June, slowly at first and then more rapidly in the seven days ending July 25. Thirty-six banks suspended with total deposits of more than $43 million. All but one – the Chicago Bank of Commerce – were small neighborhood banks located in the out-lying areas of the city. And all of the banks were relatively small: twelve had deposits of $500,000 or less, nine between $501,000 and $1 million and eleven with deposits of over $1 million and less than $6 million. We do not know whether they were closed because of panic-like depositor withdrawals or for other reasons. Neither the *Chicago Tribune* nor the *Commercial and Financial Chronicle* specifies the reasons for closing other than by action of the Board of Directors, which may mean almost anything, and "steady withdrawals." References elsewhere (see below) suggest that there were runs on the neighborhood banks as well.

However, there is no question that pandemonium broke loose on Friday, June 24 when frightened depositors converged on two large Loop banks: Continental Illinois and First Union Trust and Savings Bank. On Saturday June 25th depositors targeted the First National Bank where the run was the most intense, but there were large withdrawals from

Table 4.3   *Change in Federal Reserve notes in circulation by Federal Reserve District between June 8 and July 21, 1932*

Federal Reserve District	Federal Reserve notes in circulation ($m.)
Boston	9
New York	37
Philadelphia	9
Cleveland	6
Richmond	6
Atlanta	−1
Chicago	184
St. Louis	9
Minneapolis	7
Kansas City	11
Dallas	3
San Francisco	25
Total	305

Source: Commercial and Financial Chronicle.

Table 4.4   *Bank suspensions, deposits in failed banks, Chicago, June 15–25, 1932*

Date	Number of suspensions	Deposits in suspended banks ($m.)
June 15	1	1.3
16	3	1.4
17	1	0.5
18	4	4.2
21	5	7.5
22	6	5.9
23	7	6.5
24	5	8.9
25	4	6.3
Total	36	42.5

Source: Commercial and Financial Chronicle, June 1932, p. 4606.
Chicago Tribune, June 15–25, 1932.

Central Republic Trust as well. James (1938, pp. 103–4) described the situation on Friday and Saturday, as follows:

In the case of earlier runs, the crowds had been drawn from a particular locality or a special group: this time people from all parts of the city seemed to converge on the Loop in hysterical fear and anxiety.

In a dramatic gesture fraught with risk, Melvin Traylor, President of First National mounted a marble pillar within the bank at 11 a.m. on Saturday in the midst of excitement and confusion and managed successfully to calm the assembled crowd, and the long lines began almost immediately to evaporate. The runs were over by early afternoon.

Of the runs on the Loop banks probably the bank that suffered the most damage was Central Republic Trust created in the summer of 1931 and whose head was Charles Dawes a former Vice President of the United States, Ambassador to Great Britain, and President of the RFC. He informed Melvin Traylor and George Reynolds, the head of First National and of Continental Illinois respectively, on Sunday June 26 that the bank was not going to open on Monday morning. Aggregate deposits had fallen from $240 million in 1931 to $100 million on Saturday, June 25. Fearing that all of the Loop banks would face another dangerous run on Monday, Traylor seized the initiative in an effort to obtain assistance from the RFC to prevent the collapse of all of Chicago's banks. The RFC advanced Central Republic $90 million, the largest single loan ever extended in its short life. The size of the loan was dictated by Dawes' insistence that the sum be great enough to pay off every depositor in full. From that position he never wavered. The RFC acquiesced in what today would be recognized as the "too big to fail" defense.

Its significance will become clear later in our discussion of the banking panic of 1933 when RFC officials refused to grant a sizeable loan to two Detroit banks even though RFC officials at the time recognized that failure to grant the loans would have repercussions on the banking situation in the country as a whole. We shall have to ask what was so different about the banking difficulties in Detroit and those in Chicago that warranted discriminatory treatment? The extent of the havoc wrought on Chicago banks by the Great Depression is evident from the fact that Chicago had 225 banks in 1929. At the end of June and July 1932 that number had shrunk to sixty.

In August nine banks failed in Idaho with $11 million of deposits. The suspended banks represented only 11 percent of failed banks in August but nearly one-third of the deposits in closed banks. A run on the Boise City National Bank led to its closing on August 1. Two banks remained in the city: First Security Bank an affiliate of First Security Corporation and the Idaho First National, the lead bank in a chain of affiliated banks in Idaho. Crawford Moore, the head of Idaho First National informed the President of First Security that he intended to close all of the banks within the chain. A last minute effort was made to secure support from the RFC but to no avail. Moore insisted that the RFC advance funds on the same terms as provided to the Dawes Chicago bank in June. The RFC rejected his proposal, and Moore closed all the banks in the chain on August 31. That left First Security as the only remaining bank in Boise. A run ensued that lasted two days. The First Security's success in providing currency caused the lines of panicky depositors to collapse.

The impact of the Idaho suspension on depositor confidence was minimal if measured by Federal Reserve notes in circulation in the San Francisco Federal Reserve District. Federal Reserve notes in circulation declined by $9 million in August. The RFC loaned $2 million to the First National, and on November 1 the bank and its affiliates reopened.

The Idaho crisis was followed in November by a banking disturbance in Nevada. To ward off an imminent suspension of the Wingfield chain of banks, the governor declared a twelve-day banking holiday on November 1. The Wingfield chain of banks included twelve banks in nine Nevada cities but held more than 65 percent of the deposits within the state; its failure would have placed the other twenty-nine banks in the state in jeopardy. The governor flew to Washington in a last ditch effort to save the Wingfield chain. He requested that the RFC make a $2 million loan to the chain, but his request was rejected. That, however, was not the first request for RFC funds to shore up the Wingfield banks; the RFC had made a $5 million loan to the chain earlier in 1932. On December 14 the Wingfield group of banks closed.

December data reveal thirteen suspensions and deposit losses of $19 million for the state of Nevada. Since total suspensions for the entire San Francisco Reserve District were nineteen and deposit losses $22 million, we can conclude that the Nevada closings had negligible effects in the rest of the District in December. The Nevada holiday was a local event.

The Nevada crisis attracted national attention because of the novelty of the state's response, not because it contributed to a loss of depositor confidence on a national level. That has not been demonstrated. Nevada had been the first state to declare a bank moratorium since the onset of the banking crises of the Great Depression. Moreover, the suspension of payment by some, though not all, of Nevada's banks was an embarrassing admission of the complete ineffectiveness of the Federal Reserve and the RFC in coping with financial breakdown at the regional level. Suspension of cash payment had been the traditional pre-1914 response to banking panics. The Fed and the RFC presumably made that old-fashioned response obsolete. Imagine then the surprise generated nationwide upon learning of the action of the Nevada governor! It may also have influenced the Iowa and Louisiana governors who declared statewide holidays in January and February 1933.

Although the number of bank suspensions began to increase in October and especially in December 1932, there was no corresponding decrease in depositor confidence. Currency in circulation seasonally adjusted did not increase. There were no visible signs at the end of 1932 that portended the eruption of a major financial panic in late February and early March of 1933.

2   The gathering storm

The data on the number of bank suspensions and deposits in failed banks for January and February 1933 do not reveal an emerging banking crisis. Rather than a gathering storm, the data disclose an ebbing of banking unrest. The number of bank suspensions declined from 236 in January to 150 in February; deposits in failed banks fell by a third – from $143 million to $93 million. If that were all the information available, we would be hard pressed to conclude that a serious financial panic was in the making. But the number of bank suspensions and deposits in suspended banks in February do not include bank moratoria and deposit restrictions in effect in at least seven states. During the first four days of March there were only twenty-two bank suspensions. The March data are rendered virtually meaningless since bank moratoria and deposit withdrawal restrictions had been declared in forty-three states.

The seriousness of the developing crisis is better revealed by the behavior of weekly Federal Reserve notes in circulation (table 4.5). Hoarding increased by $580 million during the last week of February and by $635 million during the first week of March. The total increase in hoarding since the onset of the Michigan bank holiday on February 14 was more than $1.3 billion.

The increase in hoarding in late February and early March can be explained by at least two considerations. Prior banking crises during the Great Depression led to an increase in hoarding out of fear of further bank suspensions. In 1933 the closing of all banks in some states and the imposition of deposit withdrawal limitations in others also led to an increase in currency demanded for basic transactions. Unable to make payments by check, the public was forced to substitute cash and credit transactions. An increase of over $1.3 billion in Federal Reserve notes in circulation cannot be explained solely by the number of suspensions and

Table 4.5   *Federal Reserve notes in circulation*
weekly, February–March 1933 ($ million)

		Federal Reserve notes *
February	1	2,730
	8	2,773
	15	2,891
	21	3,000
	28	3,580
March	8	4,215
	15	4,292
	29	3,748

Note: * Not seasonally adjusted.
Source: Commercial and Financial Chronicle, 1933.

deposits in failed banks. The uncertainty that state officials would place limitations on deposit withdrawals generated a panic run on the banks, thereby spreading uncertainty and fear among the states.

Contributing to depositor uncertainty in January 1933 was a congressional decision to require the RFC to publish a list of loans made between February 2 and July 31, 1932. Olson (1977, p. 100) concluded: "In an economy where the slightest change in public confidence could endanger the whole banking system, the controversy surrounding the publication of RFC loans contributed materially to public fears and consequently to the weakness of the banking system." However, no acceleration in bank suspensions accompanied the publication of the list of banks to whom the RFC had made loans.

The incident that precipitated the 1933 panic was the declaration of a statewide banking holiday by the Governor of Michigan on February 14. Reverberations of the Michigan closings were not felt in the central money market but uncertainty spread quickly to surrounding states eventually engulfing banks in all parts of the country and culminating in the declaration of a national banking holiday by President Roosevelt on March 6.

A detailed narrative of the events leading up to the Michigan holiday appears in Kennedy (1973), Wigmore (1985), and Sullivan (1936); there is no need to reproduce it all here. We will include only as much of the narrative as necessary to establish the connection between the Michigan holiday and subsequent closings in the rest of the country during the succeeding three weeks, and the action taken or not taken by the banking authorities to find a solution to the Michigan crisis.

The Governor of Michigan declared a bank holiday when negotiations broke down between the RFC and the Guardian Group of banks in Detroit on the night of February 13. The Michigan holiday affected more than 500 banks with 900,000 depositors and $1.5 billion in deposits. There had been no run on any of the Detroit banks. What precipitated the crisis was the impending collapse of the Union Guardian Trust one of the two Detroit banks making up the Guardian Detroit Union Group which also included the Guardian National Bank of Commerce and thirty-one affiliated banks in sixteen Michigan cities with combined deposits of $260 million. The weakness of Union Guardian Trust had been revealed earlier when it had applied for and received a loan from the RFC in 1932. The source of its problems was an unusually heavy commitment to real estate financing. Wigmore (1985, p. 437) estimated that illiquid real estate related assets constituted over 70 percent of its total assets.

Although banking difficulties were not confined solely to the Guardian Group, they were clearly the more serious. The Detroit Bankers' Company with combined deposits of $420 million had as its nucleus the First National Bank of Detroit, the third largest bank in the country outside New York City, and forty affiliated statewide banks. Failure of Guardian Trust would have instant repercussions on depositor confidence in First National. The external network of affiliated banks of the Guardian Group and the Detroit Bankers' Company is what constituted the real threat to the stability of Michigan banking. Although the condition of the banks in the rest of the state was never at issue, the failure of either Guardian Trust or First National would spread fear and uncertainty immediately to the affiliated banks in the other cities of the state.

The RFC had attempted unsuccessfully to negotiate the terms of a loan that would have allowed Guardian Mortgage Trust to remain open and to protect the larger First National Group. On February 11 the Secretary of Commerce Roy Chapin and the Undersecretary of the Treasury Arthur Ballantine went to Detroit as representatives of the RFC at the request of President Hoover. They insisted that the Henry Ford interests, major stockholders of the bank, play a principal role in the bailout by subordinating $7.5 million in deposits and contributing $4 million in new capital to the Guardian Group. The negotiations collapsed when Henry Ford said that he expected the RFC to grant the loan without any further commitment from the Ford family. He simply did not believe that the RFC would allow Guardian Trust to fail. Moreover, he reminded Ballantine and Chapin that the RFC had approved a $90 million loan to the Dawes bank – the Central Republic Trust Company in Chicago – in June 1932 to prevent the breakdown of Chicago banking; there was no reason in his judgment why the RFC should not advance the funds to Guardian Trust.

The position of the RFC was made clear by Ballantine (1948, p. 136):

Mr. Chapin and I explained very carefully that the agreement could not legally provide loans beyond the appraised value of the collateral or supply new capital; that the saving of the Guardian Trust required the Ford participation; that its closing, and that of the First National Group which would surely follow, would paralyze business in Michigan; and that *paralysis would probably extend throughout the country.*

Nevertheless, Ford remained adamant; he would supply no new capital, and he would not subordinate his deposits. Likewise the RFC was equally steadfast in its conviction that it was not up to them to bailout the Ford interests. No further progress was possible. Finally, the Detroit Clearing House Association requested that the Governor of Michigan declare a bank holiday to begin February 14.

After a careful review of the available evidence, Wigmore (1985, pp. 443–4) concluded:

1 There were "colossal misjudgments" in the negotiations between the Guardian Group, the Ford interest, and the RFC. The demands placed on Henry Ford to support the bailout were probably excessive. Ford's expectations that the RFC would ultimately come to the rescue of Guardian Trust were wrong.
2 The Guardian National Bank of Commerce was probably solvent and justified an RFC loan. Guardian Trust was insolvent, and on purely legal grounds could not justify the loan. Wigmore thought there was little justification for closing both banks.

The causes of the breakdown of the negotiations listed by Wigmore were largely the result of personality conflicts and controversial accounting interpretations of bank insolvency. Ballantine (1948, p. 142) agreed with Wigmore about the importance of personality considerations. He did not think that the Michigan closings were inevitable. He thought that they were:

largely as a result of the stubbornness of Senator Couzens, matched by the suspicions of Henry Ford, who could not get over the thought that all was a plot against him personally. In my belief a change in the position of either would have made possible the avoidance of that critical downward move.

Senator James Couzens had collaborated with Ford in the formation of the Ford Motor Company. He eventually sold his interest to Ford and entered politics being elected to the US Senate from Michigan in 1922. According to Kennedy (1973, p. 86) they quarreled frequently over political issues and who should control the Detroit banks. Highly arbitrary valuations of collateral by RFC examiners also played a role in shaping the decision of how much could be loaned to Guardian Trust. Current market value was too harsh, but the alternatives were highly subjective.

But these were proximate and not the ultimate cause of the collapse of negotiations. The RFC's refusal to support the Guardian Group of banks lies in its failure to recognize a responsibility for maintaining the stability of the US banking system. The Fed had abdicated its role to guarantee financial stability by inaction and by confusion over the functions of the RFC. And officials of the RFC never acknowledged that they had a vacuum to fill by the Fed's reluctance to act as the lender of last resort. They behaved as though they were either unconcerned about the repercussions of a collapse of the Michigan banks on the rest of the country or that purely technical legal considerations (restriction on RFC loans to insolvent banks and the limitations of financial assistance to the value of the bank's collateral) were treated as an impenetrable barrier not to be breached even at the expense of contributing to a nationwide panic. To have insisted on the sanctity of legal stipulations at such a time is to have feared the wrath of the courts more than the wrath of those who would suffer economic loss; it reveals an inordinate respect for the law and an inordinate disrespect for the consequences of an impending financial catastrophe. There are ample precedents for disregarding the strict letter of the law during financial panics. We need look no further than the suspension of specie payment by US banks during nineteenth-century panics. And to the suspension by the Bank of England of the note issue constraint imposed by the 1844 Banking Act during financial panics. At the very least financial exigency should be given a fair hearing before committing to a slavish regard for the letter of the law. Legal sanction need not have preceded action if legislation followed close behind. Understandably, RFC decisionmakers might have been confused about their lender-of-last-resort responsibilities. They, perhaps, paid too much attention to assisting individual distressed banks – provided, of course, that the bank was solvent – and too little attention to the solvency of the banking system generally.

The declaration of a bank holiday by the Michigan governor on February 14 was not a new remedy for an impending banking crisis. Sprague (1910, p. 286) and Andrew (1908, pp. 434–6) reported that governors of five Western states – Oklahoma, Nevada, Washington, Oregon, and California – had declared a succession of legal holidays during the panic of 1907. Sprague noted specifically that the bank holiday was a "novel device" for coping with banking crises. But it had been used locally in Chicago (1871), Boston (1872), Baltimore (1904), and San Francisco (1906) in the aftermath of serious fires (Upham and Lamke, 1934, pp. 9–11). Oregon passed a law in 1930 allowing the officers of a bank to suspend payments for sixty days. Florida allowed banks with the approval of the Comptroller of Banks to limit deposit withdrawals to 20 percent. Similar legislation was passed in Massachusetts, Michigan, and Virginia in 1932. During the first five months of 1932, 658 banks in twenty-two states were forced to restrict payment to depositors to keep from closing, 150 of which were located in the three states of Michigan, Minnesota, and Texas (Study Commission for Indiana Financial Institutions, 1932, p. 83).

The declaration of the Michigan holiday spread fear and uncertainty quickly to the contiguous states of Ohio, Indiana, and Illinois who promptly placed restrictions on deposit withdrawals. Cleveland banks experienced heavy withdrawals. The increase in banking unrest in the fourth and seventh Federal Reserve Districts following the Michigan bank suspension is revealed in the changes in note circulation, bills discounted, and securities and acceptances purchased by the two District banks. Bills discounted, bills bought, and government securities increased $44 million (20 percent) between February 15 and February 28 in the Cleveland District. Federal Reserve notes in circulation increased by $77 million (24 percent). The increase in the Chicago District was equally impressive. Notes in circulation increased by $117 million (15 percent). And bills discounted, bills bought, and securities purchased increased by over $200 million between February 15 and February 28. What is especially noteworthy is that the Chicago Fed on its own initiative purchased nearly $100 million of government securities. The purchases were made by the bank and were not authorized by the Open Market Policy Conference. Eighty-two million dollars of bankers' acceptances were also acquired by the bank. Bills discounted increased by only $24 million. The response of the Chicago Fed was prompt and on a scale that speaks well for the Chicago Bank leadership, but they played a negative role in resolving the crisis in Detroit.

During the two weeks following the closing of the Michigan banks, there was intense activity on the part of the officials of the two closed Detroit banks, the RFC, the Federal Reserve Bank of Chicago, and the Comptroller of the Currency to devise a workable plan for reorganizing the Guardian National and the First National banks. The view of all concerned seemed to be that the two existing banks could not simply be reopened; there were serious doubts about their solvency. It would be necessary to attempt to establish either one or two new banks with new charters and new capital structures and to determine how much should be paid to the depositors of the old banks and where the funds were to come from.

During the first week following the announcement of the bank holiday, the president of First National approached the Federal Reserve Bank of Chicago about a 10-A loan of $35 million. The Glass–Steagall Act of 1932 (Public Law No. 44) amended the Federal Reserve Act by adding a new section (10-A) to empower Federal Reserve Banks with the approval of not less than five members of the Federal Reserve Board to make advances to groups of five or more member banks upon their time or demand promissory notes provided these banks had no adequate amount of eligible and acceptable assets available to obtain normal accommodation. The banks receiving assistance must deposit with a suitable trustee their individual notes backed by as much collateral as may be agreed upon. Advances could be made to banks in groups of less than five if the aggregate amount of their deposit liability constituted at least 10 percent of the entire deposit liability of all member banks within each District. The purpose of the loan to the First National was to help in opening a new bank with a 50 percent payment to depositors. The initial expectations were that the bank would obtain a $100 million loan from the RFC, $17.5 million in new capital from local sources, $20 million from New York bankers, and $5 million in rediscounts from the Chicago Fed. Since the New York bankers had refused to participate, the officials of First National requested $35 million from the Chicago Fed.

Minutes of the Chicago Fed (Stevens, 1934, p. 5819) for February 20 show that the directors were not inclined to lend such a sum to a closed bank that was not likely to reopen. They stated that it would "establish a dangerous precedent," and it would be more desirable to conserve their resources for existing member banks. They gave as one of their reasons the questionable legality of making loans to a closed bank that did not intend to reopen by payment to depositors the full amount of their deposits. Thus ended the opportunity of the Federal Reserve Bank of Chicago to aid in the reopening of the larger of the two Detroit banks. The Guardian Group apparently made no effort to obtain assistance from the Chicago Fed, and the Chicago Fed took no initiative to aid the bank.

Kennedy's (1973, p. 99) account of what happened differs from that of Eugene Stevens (1934, pp. 5811–28) Chairman of the Federal Reserve Bank of Chicago and Federal Reserve Agent. Kennedy stated that First National's application for the 10-A loan failed because its eligible paper had not yet been exhausted, and it could not obtain a cosigner of the loan. I am baffled by the latter constraint. There is nothing in section

10-A of the Glass–Steagall Act that requires the borrowing bank to obtain a cosigner of the loan! After the application failed, she stated that the officers of the First National decided that they could reopen on a 50 percent basis if they obtained assistance from the RFC, the Federal Reserve Bank of Chicago, and the New York banks. But according to Stevens (1934, p. 5817) there was no formal application for a loan by First National, only a desire to obtain the Fed's reaction. He says that the officers of the First National approached the Fed for the first time on Friday, February 18 for a $35 million 10-A loan, and he repeated what they said was the purpose of the loan: to reopen on a 50 percent basis if they could obtain a $100 million loan for a new bank from the RFC. According to Stevens (1933, p. 5817) their request for a $35 million loan was made only after they had heard from the New York banks that they would not make the loan. Stevens read to the Pecora Committee an excerpt from the Chicago Fed minutes dated February 20, 1933 in which the directors said they believed it unwise for the bank to *entertain* such a loan, thereby indicating that the bank had no formal application from the First National Bank. The "dangerous precedent" they did not wish to set was advancing funds to a closed bank that could not pay its depositors in full and in all likelihood would not reopen under its old charter. No mention was made either that the First National's eligible paper had been exhausted or that it had failed to obtain a cosigner of the loan!

Plans to reorganize the two banks with RFC assistance were continuously under consideration until February 28. The Governor of Michigan extended the bank holiday indefinitely on February 21. At a meeting of the RFC on February 22, there was tentative agreement to set up two new banks with an injection of local capital funds and a $35 million adequately secured loan to Guardian National Bank and $100 million loan to First National. Secretary of the Treasury Ogden Mills (1934, p. 4748) said "that it was absolutely essential to avert the collapse of the banking structure in the important cities mentioned [Detroit and Cleveland]." On February 25, the RFC agreed to lend First National $90 million and Guardian National $35 million to carry out their reorganization allowing depositors 30 percent of their unsecured deposits contingent upon their obtaining $20 million in loans from New York banks and approximately $4.4 million from the Chicago Fed. Negotiations broke down when the New York banks refused to make the loan.

On the 26th the RFC reduced substantially the loan request of both First National and Guardian National; it was prepared to lend First National $54 million and Guardian National $24 million contingent upon adequate capital being made available. The RFC gave the officials of the two banks an ultimatum to respond by 6.00 p.m. Edsel and Henry Ford made a dramatic announcement before the ultimatum expired. They agreed to put up the necessary capital of $8,250,000 to establish two new banks if they were given discretion to select an entirely new management team. Almost all of the officers of the two banks would be retired. The shareholders presumably accepted the terms of the Fords' proposal, and the two reorganized banks were scheduled to open on February 27 and March 2 respectively with an agreed payout of 30 cents on the dollar. But for reasons that have never been fully revealed, the bankers reneged on their initial agreement. On February 28 the chairman of the First National Bank notified the RFC that it would be inadvisable to go ahead with the plan proposed by the Fords. Thus ended all efforts to resolve the Michigan crisis before the declaration of a national holiday on March 6.

The proffered solutions to the Michigan crisis were not confined solely to establishing one or two new Detroit banks. Additional proposals included a plan to issue Clearing House scrip under the direction of the Federal Reserve Banks. Each member bank would make scrip available to individual depositors immediately on a pro rata basis equal to the value of the bank's good assets. This was known as the Hoover plan or the Detroit scrip plan and was initiated by President Hoover on February 14. The plan was opposed strongly by Governors Meyer and Harrison of the Federal Reserve on the grounds that the issue of scrip would reflect negatively on the "adequacy and flexibility" of the Federal Reserve. The next day February 15 there was another discussion of the scrip plan at the Treasury attended by George Davison, chairman of the New York Clearing House Association and who had handled the issue of scrip in the panic of 1907, Secretary of the Treasury Mills, and Governor Harrison of the Federal Reserve Bank of New York. According to Sullivan (1936, p. 90) it was decided to introduce the scrip plan in Detroit. However, no reference is given for the source of this information. Considering the declared opposition of both Governors Meyer and Harrison to the issue of scrip, there is some question about whether such a decision was actually made. Of course, the Secretary of the Treasury had the authority to implement the decision with or without the cooperation of the Federal Reserve. But it would not have been in keeping with Hoover's distaste for imposing a decision on a recalcitrant Fed.

The second proposal called for closing the banks one afternoon and reopening them the next morning, each depositor receiving a pro-rated credit representing his share in the bank's net assets. This plan was recommended by Governors Meyer and Harrison. It was referred to as the New York plan or the Broderick plan (Superintendent of Banking for the State of New York). The measure would have had to receive the approval of the Michigan legislature which at a minimum would have taken ten days. The consideration of such a proposal publicly would have encouraged the immediate withdrawal of deposits thus exacerbating the banking crisis.

The Hoover scrip proposal was rejected by the Federal Reserve. The Broderick plan got nowhere because of the projected delays in obtaining the requisite legislation. And the merger proposals were stillborn because of RFC insistence that new capital be raised as a condition for granting a loan, the inability to win the support of the New York creditor banks, and the opposition of Michigan's powerful Senator Couzens who by subtle intimidation was able to torpedo the proposal to establish a new bank. He claimed that the proposal favored city banks at the expense of country banks, and he threatened to bring the whole matter to the floor of the Senate where the effects of a full Senate debate on depositor confidence could not be readily foreseen. By March 1 it was too late. The problem was now national in scope – not how to reopen the Michigan banks but how to contain a nationwide panic in the form of the declaration of bank holidays in the several states.

The period between the closing of the Michigan banks and the declaration of a national bank holiday has to be the most exasperating two and a half weeks in twentieth century financial history. No agreement could be reached about the conditions for reopening the Michigan banks. As a result, the crisis repercussions spread rapidly to more than thirty states. If there had been bold and effective action initially to reopen the Michigan banks, the collapse of the banking system may have been averted. There was no deficiency of plans to reopen the Michigan banks and restore depositor confidence. What was lacking was the element of leadership that would have commanded the cooperation of the interested parties. Neither President Hoover, the Federal Reserve, the RFC, nor the bankers themselves had the necessary clout to impose a viable solution to the Michigan crisis. Hoover, perhaps, had the clout but was reluctant to impose an arbitrary solution on unwilling participants. No individual actor in the drama had adequate recognition of the costs of failure to act: personality quirks, agency pride, legal technicalities, and old fashioned politics took precedence over public interest considerations. How else can we explain endless discussion and delay over what should be done while banking activity in several states came to a virtual standstill? It would not be unreasonable to conclude that the proposed remedies were regarded as worse than the disease. But it is difficult to see how the adoption of any of the projected remedies would be worse than a total banking collapse. The participants either did not perceive a banking collapse or they underestimated its probable effects.

The effect of the Michigan banking crisis was to shift the burden of responsibility for doing something about bank suspensions from unsuccessful national endeavors on the part of the President, the Reconstruction Financial Corporation (RFC), and the Federal Reserve to the individual states who, under existing legislative mandates, were ill-equipped to assume their new responsibilities. Legislation was drafted and passed at breakneck speed to meet the threat of the deteriorating banking situation. Governors and state banking officials were immediately empowered to close all banks within a state, limit deposit withdrawals, or allow directors of individual banks at their discretion to declare temporary moratoria and limit withdrawals. The latter annulled previous time-honored regulations that forced a bank into receivership if it was not able to pay depositors on demand. State banking officials were given what amounted to dictatorial powers to control the banks.

This last illustrates only too well how badly the banking situation had worsened. No confidence remained in the national authorities – the RFC, the Federal Reserve, and the President – to exercise the requisite leadership and initiative to bring the situation under control. Each state reacted to protect its own interests without regard to its effects on others. Abdication of national responsibility led to a scramble on the part of the individual states to attempt to reduce the damage of bank closings to a minimum.

Limitations on deposit withdrawal was an abrogation of the established rule "first come, first serve" in the allocation of deposits to panic-ridden depositors. By placing a ceiling on deposit withdrawals, there would be a more equitable distribution of deposits without endangering the solvency of the banks. Banks could remain open to satisfy the emergency needs of their customers. Bank officials were not required by law to impose withdrawal limits; that was left to the discretion of the directors or other officers of the banks.

On February 21 New York and New Jersey both passed laws allowing individual banks to place restrictions on the percentage of deposit balances that could be withdrawn. On February 23 the Governor of Indiana signed into law a bill that gave sweeping new powers to the state banking department including the power to limit withdrawals from individual banks or groups of banks. Directors of individual banks could restrict deposit withdrawal at any time after appropriate notice had been given. And on February 26 the Indianapolis Clearing House Association limited withdrawals on all deposits to 5 percent. Following the announcement of the Indianapolis Clearing House, banks in other Indiana cities introduced similar restrictions. Missouri passed a bank moratorium bill on February 25 which gave officers of state banks and trust companies authority to declare six-day moratoria when unusual withdrawals were made or were about to be made. Ohio passed enabling legislation on February 27 to allow banking officials to control the withdrawal of deposits ostensibly to curtail out-of-state withdrawals and to ward off the necessity to declare a bank holiday. Almost immediately thereafter the Cleveland Stock Exchange closed. Banks in Cleveland, Columbus, Akron, Dayton, and Youngstown introduced deposit withdrawal limits. And on February 28 both the Pennsylvania and West Virginia legislatures gave individual banks the right to limit deposit withdrawals; in Pennsylvania the state secretary of banking was granted the authority to fix the withdrawal percentage. Governor Pinchot stated that the purpose of the resolution passed by the legislature was to make a moratorium unnecessary.

During the final week of February, at least seven states passed legislation authorizing banks to limit deposit withdrawals. In three of the seven (Ohio, Indiana, Pennsylvania) withdrawal restrictions went into effect immediately in some of the larger cities. The Governor of Maryland declared a bank holiday on the 25th. The immediate response, therefore, to the Michigan closing was the imposition of deposit withdrawals in seventeen states and a bank moratorium in one.

On March 1 banking holidays were declared in California tying up nearly $3 billion of depositors, Kentucky, Tennessee, Alabama, and Louisiana. The next day bank moratoria went in to effect in Nevada, Oregon, Alabama, Arizona, Washington, and Mississippi. March 3 saw the extension to five more states: Utah, Idaho, Wisconsin, Georgia, and New Mexico. Bank closings were not mandatory in Kentucky, Alabama, and Arizona. Between February 14 and March 3 banking holidays of various durations were in effect in eighteen states, seven were in contiguous Western states and four in contiguous Southern states. Withdrawal restrictions were in effect in an additional twelve states: Ohio, Indiana, Illinois, Pennsylvania, New Jersey, Delaware, Arkansas, Texas, Missouri, West Virginia, Minnesota, and Kansas.

The panic that was sweeping the country during the last week of February and the first three days of March was a panic generated by officials in the several states who either declared bank holidays or limited deposit withdrawals. It was not depositor runs on the banks in the classic sense that prompted such drastic measures. Rather it was an unwillingness on the part of state officials to stand idly by while depositors attempted to transfer funds to surrounding states where deposit restrictions were not in effect.

By the time Roosevelt was inaugurated on March 4, 1933 banks had been either closed (or deposits restricted) in forty-eight states. The status of banking restrictions is shown below in thirty-three states, deposit withdrawals restricted in ten, and optional closings in five. Prior to the issuance of the proclamation of President Roosevelt providing for a nationwide bank holiday the *New York Times* printed the following in its issue of March 5:

Limitations on banking are shown State by State in the following compilation by The Associated Press:

ALABAMA – Closed until further notice.

ARIZONA – Closed until March 13.

ARKANSAS – Closed until March 7.

CALIFORNIA – Almost all closed until March 9.

COLORADO – Closed until March 8.

CONNECTICUT – Closed until March 7.

DELAWARE – Closed indefinitely.

DISTRICT OF COLUMBIA – Three banks limited to 5%; nine savings banks invoke sixty days' notice.

FLORIDA – Withdrawals restricted to 5%; plus $10 until March 8.

GEORGIA – Mostly closed until March 7, closing optional.

IDAHO – Some closed until March 18, closing optional.

ILLINOIS – Closed until March 8, then to be opened on 5% restriction basis for seven days.

INDIANA – About half restricted to 5% indefinitely.

IOWA – Closed "temporarily."

KANSAS – Restricted to 5% withdrawals indefinitely.

KENTUCKY – Mostly restricted to 5% withdrawals until March 11.

LOUISIANA – Closing mandatory until March 7.

MAINE – Closed until March 7.

MARYLAND – Closed until March 6.

MASSACHUSETTS – Closed until March 7.

MICHIGAN – Mostly closed, others restricted to 5% indefinitely; Upper Peninsula banks open.

MINNESOTA – Closed "temporarily."

MISSISSIPPI – Restricted to 5% indefinitely.

MISSOURI – Closed until March 7.

MONTANA – Closed until further notice.

NEBRASKA – Closed until March 8.

NEVADA – Closed until March 8, also schools.

NEW HAMPSHIRE – Closed subject to further proclamation.

NEW JERSEY – Closed until March 7.

NEW MEXICO – Mostly closed until March 8.

NEW YORK – Closed until March 7.

NORTH CAROLINA – Some Banks restricted to 5% withdrawals.

NORTH DAKOTA – Closed temporarily.

OHIO – Mostly restricted to 5% withdrawals indefinitely.

OKLAHOMA – All closed until March 8.

OREGON – All closed until March 7.

PENNSYLVANIA – Mostly closed until March 7, Pittsburgh banks open.

RHODE ISLAND – Closed yesterday.

SOUTH CAROLINA – Some closed, some restricted, all on own initiative.

SOUTH DAKOTA – Closed indefinitely.

TENNESSEE – A few closed, others restricted, until March 9.

TEXAS – Mostly closed, other restricted to withdrawals of $15 daily until March 8.

UTAH – Mostly closed until March 8.

VERMONT – Closed until March 7.

VIRGINIA – All closed until March 8.

WASHINGTON – Some closed until March 7.

WEST VIRGINIA – Restricted to 5% monthly withdrawals indefinitely.

WISCONSIN – Closed until March 17.

WYOMING – Withdrawals restricted to 5% indefinitely.

His proclamation declaring a nationwide banking holiday to commence March 6 was simply a recognition of what had already occurred as a result of uncoordinated action by the several governors and state legislatures. A nationwide bank holiday transferred the power to reopen the banks from the state to the Federal government. But the proclamation was more than a declaration of a bank holiday to cope with the internal drain of currency; it was equally an attempt to cope with an external drain that had reached dangerous proportions. The exporting or earmarking of gold and silver bullion was made illegal during the initial four-day holiday. Moreover, the Secretary of the Treasury with the approval of the President was empowered to permit the issuance of Clearing House Certificates or other evidence of claims against the assets of banking institutions. On March 9, Roosevelt extended the bank holiday and gold embargo indefinitely.

3   The external drain

The rapidly deteriorating banking situation can easily be taken as the principal, if not the only, reason for the declaration of the national banking holiday. But there was a serious external drain as well. The gold reserves of the Federal Reserve Banks fell from $3,255 million on February 1 to $2,684 million on March 8 – a decrease of $571 million. If we include the $151 million decline in the US Treasury's gold custody account at the Federal Reserve Bank of New York, the total gold loss amounted to $735 million, roughly the equivalent of the gold loss in October 1931. The gold drain accelerated after Michigan declared a bank moratorium on February 14, accounting for more than 70 percent of the total losses since February 1.

The seriousness of the gold loss is not evident when we consider the total gold holdings of the twelve Federal Reserve Banks. But the losses of the New York Fed were becoming critical. Between February 1 and March 8 the New York Fed lost 60 percent of its gold reserve. By March 4, only $381 million remained. Considering that foreign deposits alone amounted to over $600 million in New York City, the prospects for maintaining convertibility of gold looked slim. Barrie Wigmore (1987, p. 745) obtained daily figures from the archives of the New York Fed revealing the full extent of the gold loss on a daily basis. These are the figures quoted above.

To bolster the New York Bank's position, the Chicago Fed loaned the New York Fed $105 million on March 1 and another $60 million on March 2 which together with increased discounts and advances reduced the reserve ratio of the Chicago Fed to 56 percent; it had been as high as 80 percent two weeks earlier. When confronted with an additional request for $150 million on March 3, the request was refused on the grounds that the Chicago Bank's position would be seriously weakened. To prevent the transfer of funds James (1938, pp. 1062–3) states that Edward Brown of the First National Bank of Chicago threatened to present $75 million of Federal Reserve notes to the Chicago Fed for redemption in gold. He invited the other Chicago bankers to do the same. Governor McDougal of the Federal Reserve Bank of Chicago countered by stating that the Fed would call the loans of any member bank that attempted to convert Federal Reserve notes into gold. The First National, however, was not indebted to the Fed. McDougal had to accept a compromise. Brown would not present the Federal Reserve notes for redemption if McDougal would deny New York's request for funds. Although the Federal Reserve Board had the authority to order Chicago to supply the requested funds, it did not do so for what reasons we do not know. Nevertheless, we do know that the Board was considering a suspension of the gold reserve requirement which it put into effect on March 3. Wigmore (1987, p. 747) states that "The spirit in Chicago appears to have been at work in some other Federal Reserve districts: The Richmond, St. Louis, Minneapolis, Kansas City, and Dallas Federal Reserve Banks all increased their gold holdings between February 15 and March 8." He concluded that the New York Bank was alone in facing the increased demands for gold.

Wigmore (1985) and Donaldson (1992) have concluded that external, not internal, considerations were primarily responsible for Roosevelt's action in declaring a national bank holiday. They both considered the gold reserve position of the New York Fed as paramount, not the contagion of fear among depositors. Nor was the problem insufficient liquidity of New York and Chicago commercial banks. Bankers in New York and Chicago wanted no part of a bank moratorium or deposit restriction scheme; they felt that they could withstand the increased pressure of further out-of-town withdrawals since the increase in bank moratoria in individual states had almost eliminated the demand of the interior banks for funds. Nevertheless, they reluctantly went along with the request of the governors of New York and Chicago to close the banks.

But it does not follow that the timing of the national banking holiday proclaimed by Roosevelt on March 6 was dictated solely, or even primarily, by the external drain and the condition of the New York Federal Reserve Bank. What Wigmore has shown is the primacy of the external drain in accounting for Governor Lehman's decision to close the banks in New York State on March 3. The banking system had collapsed before Roosevelt was inaugurated president on March 4 and was in complete disarray, even if New York and Chicago bankers preferred to remain open. Banks in thirty-three states had been closed temporarily and deposits restricted in ten. Some of these banks were scheduled to be reopened on March 6, most on March 7 or 8. There were no prospects that such a schedule could have been adhered to. No plans or strategies existed in the states to put their banking houses in order. Without national leadership, the individual states could do little or nothing. Uncoordinated state initiatives had led to the debacle. And uncoordinated state initiatives could not provide a remedy for a national crisis.

The timing of the national banking holiday was dictated by two considerations simultaneously: a banking system that had collapsed without any prospects for recovery unless there was an assertion of national leadership, and an external drain that was threatening the convertibility of the dollar into gold. Roosevelt's proclamation on March 6 recognized the priority of both of these considerations:

Whereas there have been heavy and unwarranted withdrawals of gold and currency from our banking institutions for the purpose of hoarding; and
Whereas continuous and increasingly extensive speculation actively abroad in foreign exchanges has resulted in severe drains on the nation's stock of gold; and
Whereas these conditions have created a national emergency, and
Whereas it is in the best interests of all bank depositors that a period of respite be provided with a view to preventing further hoarding of coins, bullion or currency,

or speculation on foreign exchange and permitting the application of appropriate measures to protect the interests of the people ...

Wigmore regarded the timing of the national banking holiday as a riddle. But, as I have attempted to show, there was nothing puzzling about the timing of Roosevelt's proclamation. Both officials of the outgoing Hoover administration and Roosevelt's advisers agreed that a bank holiday was essential to halt further deterioration of the banking situation. Hoover felt a bank holiday was necessary but would not issue such a proclamation without Roosevelt's approval. And Roosevelt was not willing to accept responsibility before he was inaugurated. If there ever was a riddle about timing, it was why the holiday had not been declared earlier by Hoover not why it was one of the first acts of the new administration.

4   Money and the capital market during the panic

Unlike nineteenth-century financial panics, there is no evidence of a credit squeeze in the New York money market during the 1933 crisis. New York City banks were flush with liquidity and were reluctant converts to a bank moratorium. Large Chicago banks were equally loath to request a moratorium. That is not to say that there were not considerable strains placed on the Chicago banks. Between February 15 and March 8 net demand deposits declined by $177 million, over $100 million of which occurred between March 1 and March 3. Friday, March 3 was the worst day. There were runs on outlying banks and huge withdrawals of funds by corporations and individuals in Loop banks in anticipation of a moratorium. Credit nevertheless was available in the New York and Chicago money markets throughout the crisis at reasonable rates.

There was a moderate increase in interest rates before the declaration of a national bank holiday on March 6 but only in rates on prime bankers' acceptances and new stock exchange loans and that did not occur until after February 25 (table 4.6). The increase was barely over 100 basis points, a relatively mild increase considering the incipient breakdown of the banking system. Surprisingly enough, weekly averages of daily rates show no change in the four–six month commercial paper rate which had remained unchanged at 1.38 percent since January 7. Nevertheless, if we refer to the daily rates, there was an increase to 3 percent on Friday, March 3.

The New York Fed put up the discount rate from 2 1/2 to 3 1/2 percent on March 3 which was followed by only one other Federal Reserve Bank – St. Louis on March 4. Considering that banks had been

Table 4.6   *Select short-term interest rates weekly, January–March 1933*

		Prime commercial paper 4-6 month	Prime bankers' acceptances	New stock exchange loans
Jan.	7	1.38	0.38	1.00
	14	1.38	0.38	1.00
	21	1.38	0.38	1.00
	28	1.38	0.25	1.00
Feb.	4	1.38	0.25	1.00
	11	1.38	0.25	1.00
	18	1.38	0.44	1.00
	25	1.38	0.63	1.00
March	4	1.38	2.25	2.06
	11*	——	——	——
	18	4.25	3.25	4.31
	25	3.25	2.00	3.00

Note: * Bank Holiday.
Source: Board of Governors of Federal Reserve System, *Banking and Monetary Statistics*, 1914–1941, Washington DC, August 1976.

closed in thirty-three states and withdrawals severely restricted in most others by March 4, the rate increase could hardly be regarded by past standards of performance of panic proportions. Since markets were shut down during the week March 4–March 11, no rate quotations are available. Nevertheless, rate quotations for March 18 show substantial increases over their March 4 levels: over 300 basis points for the commercial paper rate, 100 basis points for prime bankers' acceptances, and 200 basis points for new stock exchange loans.

The Treasury had issued $101 million of ninety-one day bills on February 27 at 0.99 percent, up from 0.55 percent a week earlier. On March 3 there was an additional issue of $75 million of ninety-three day bills, but by this time the rate had increased to 4.26 percent. Call loan rates had advanced from 1 to 2 percent on March 1, to 2 1/2 percent on March 2, and to 3 1/2 percent on March 3.

The run up of rates was also reflected in the bond market. Moody's bond yield averages for 120 domestic bonds are shown in table 4.7. Aaa rated bond yields increased from 4.43 percent on February 14 to 4.81 percent on March 3. That represented a 6 percent price decline. Baa bond yields rose form 8.22 percent to 9.27 percent, an equivalent price decline of 12 percent. When markets reopened on March 15, Aaa rated bond yields fell to 4.7 percent and Baa to 8.87 percent.

Table 4.7   *Moody's rated bond yield averages daily, February 15–March 3, 1933*

		All 120 Domestic	Aaa	Baa
Feb.	15	6.03	4.43	8.22
	16	6.08	4.46	8.29
	17	6.10	4.48	8.31
	18	6.13	4.48	8.39
	20	6.19	4.51	8.47
	21	6.26	4.53	8.56
	23	6.37	4.59	8.73
	24	6.32	4.57	8.68
	25	6.41	4.61	8.83
	27	6.50	4.65	9.02
	28	6.51	4.67	9.03
March	1	6.54	4.71	9.04
	2	6.65	4.79	9.22
	3	6.70	4.81	9.27

Source: Commercial and Financial Chronicle, 1933.

The explanation for the relatively mild run up in short-term rates can be found in the Fed's strategy for supplying reserves. Between February 15 and March 8 currency in circulation had increased by $1.7 billion, and the monetary gold stock decreased by $268 million (table 4.8). If not offset, reserve deposits would have fallen by $2 billion. The Fed pursued a liberal discount policy with discounts and advances increasing by over $1.1 billion; bills bought increased $400 million for a total reserve injection of $1.5 billion. Reserve deposits fell by half a billion dollars. However, the monetary base increased by $1.2 billion.

5   The Fed's response to the gathering storm

The open market policy in effect in mid February had been approved at a meeting of the Open Market Policy Conference (OMPC) on January 4, 1933. A target level of excess reserves was set at $500 million (Wicker, 1966, pp. 186–7). And a ceiling was placed on the amount of government security holdings in the investment account; they were not to rise above $1,851 million without reconvening the OMPC. The alleged reasons for placing a ceiling on the security portfolio was a fear that additional reserves might force the banks to suspend interest payments on demand

Table 4.8   *Determinants of reserve deposits, February 15–March 8, 1933 ($m.)*

	Feb. 15	March 8	Change
Bills discounted	286	1,414	1,128
Bills bought	31	417	386
US government securities	1,809	1,881	72
All other securities	10	−68	−58
Total	2,136	3,644	1,508
Gold stock	4,224	3,956	−268
Treasury currency	2,203	2,230	27
Currency in circulation	5,567	' 7,251	1,684
Treasury cash	278	279	1
Treasury deposits at Fed.	52	38	−14
Nonmember deposits	88	138	50
Other reserve accounts	342	348	6
Reserve deposits	2,236	1,776	−460
Monetary base	5,567	7,251	
Total	7,803	9,027	1,224

Source: Board of Governors of the Federal Reserve System, *Banking and Monetary Statistics, 1914–1941*, Washington DC, August 1976.

deposits and thereby increase hoarding. Moreover, further increases in excess reserves might impair bank earnings.

Table 4.9 shows member bank indebtedness, government securities, currency in circulation, and excess reserves of member banks weekly from January 4 to March 8, 1933. At the time of the Michigan holiday excess reserves had fallen well below the targeted level, and the security portfolio had reached the agreed upon ceiling. On February 16 the New York Fed lowered the bill rate to 1/2 percent because of the constraint on security purchases. The New York Bank officials accomplished through the purchase of bills and increased borrowing what they could not through the purchase of government securities. On February 20 the excess reserves of the New York banks disappeared; there was no option other than to lower bill rates to inject additional reserves. Nevertheless, excess reserves remained below the targeted level through March 8.

There is no question that the New York Bank would have pursued a vigorous policy of open market operations if the constraint on the security portfolio had been absent. They were able, however, to accomplish partly through their bill buying strategy what they could not accomplish through open market operations.

Table 4.9 *Member bank indebtedness, government securities held by Federal Reserve Banks, currency in circulation, and excess reserves of member banks weekly* from January 4 to March 8, 1933 $ million*

1933		Bills discounted	Government securities	Currency in circulation	Excess reserves
January	1	251	1,851	5,383	582
	11	248	1,812	5,302	627
	18	249	1,778	5,315	609
	25	265	1,763	5,324	573
February	1	269	1,764	5,365	499
	8	253	1,784	5,418	501
	15	286	1,809	5,567	340
	22	327	1,834	5,701	401
March	1	712	1,836	6,432	272
	8	1,414	1,881	7,251	129

Note: *Wednesday figures.
Source: Board of Governors of the Federal Reserve System, *Banking and Monetary Statistics*, Washington DC, 1976, p. 387.

A conflict arose between action to inject reserves through lowering of bill rates and the inevitable tendency for rates to rise owing to domestic hoarding and the export of gold. New York Bank officials were concerned increasingly with the posted bill rates being out of touch with the market, and on February 27 they advanced the bill rate to 1 percent. Two questions remain to be answered: why no meeting was called to obtain authority for increased purchases of securities, and would increased purchases have forestalled the total collapse of the banking system?

Governor Harrison did not believe that there was sufficient support among the members of the OMPC for additional purchases because of the disposition of some governors at the January meeting to allow the securities portfolio to run down without replacement. Harrison (Discussion Notes, February 23, 1933, p. 84) told the New York directors on February 23 that "our partners would not go along." And again on the 27th he said that he had been in Washington the day before to discuss the situation with Governor Meyer of the Federal Reserve Board and Secretary of the Treasury Ogden Mills. They both agreed "it would be futile, at this time, to attempt or to consider further purchases of government securities" (Discussion Notes, February 27, 1933, p. 188). Moreover, Governor Harrison made it quite clear that he would not recommend purchases unless the Chicago and Boston Reserve Banks agreed to participate. Considering the rapidly deteriorating condition of the New York Bank's gold reserve ratio, there was a sound basis for Harrison's demand that Boston and Chicago participate as well.

Governor Harrison and the New York Fed deserve credit for having exercised initiative in preventing a panic in the New York money market by supplying needed reserves through the bill market when security purchases were not feasible and to have cushioned the impact on reserves of gold exports. There is no evidence to support the contention that Governor Meyer and the other Board members in Washington would have exercised the requisite leadership in the absence of Harrison's initiatives. If Harrison had had the authority to have acted alone, security purchases probably would have been more generous, but how much more generous it is not possible to say since he was equally concerned about the possibility that hoarding might increase if banks refused to pay interest on demand balances, and later the decline in the New York Bank's free gold. The New York money market was able to withstand the strains of gold withdrawals right up to the last and the exodus of funds to the interior largely through the efforts of the New York Fed. Much of the pressure, however, had been relieved by the declaration of moratoria in thirty-three states. The Fed deserves full credit for successfully preventing a panic in the central money market by providing for a smooth transfer of funds between New York and the interior without immoderate increases in interest rates, even at the panic's peak. This was accomplished without resorting to open market operations. Moreover, banks in both New York and Chicago remained highly liquid and solvent. Nevertheless, stability in the central money market did not reduce instability elsewhere.

What the Fed failed to do was maintain the solvency of the banking system outside New York and Chicago. What, we might ask, might the Fed have done differently? The Open Market Policy Conference (OMPC) conceivably could have engaged in open market operations on a far grander scale than in 1932 when the OMPC purchased $1 billion of government securities, the results of which were to increase excess reserves without stimulating either new lending or deposit expansion. Much larger purchases may have been necessary in February to satiate the banks' demand for excess reserves. Large purchases, moreover, may have contributed to restoring depositor confidence by demonstrating Fed leadership. On the other hand, these favorable effects may have been offset if foreign investors had responded by exchanging dollar assets for gold.

What Fed officials could have done differently was to recognize its lender-of-last-resort responsibilities and extended its support to troubled banks even if they were of questionable solvency with insufficient collateral and whose demise would spread fear and uncertainty to other banks in the rest of the country. There was no solid basis for their having relinquished their lender-of-last-resort responsibilities to the RFC. The banking situation in Detroit clearly called for whatever action was necessary to prevent the collapse of the Michigan banks.

Whether a more vigorous open market policy coupled with a policy to shore up larger banks in difficulty would have been successful is not certain. But the Fed would have done all that it could ideally have been expected to do. The ideal policy, as we have attempted to show, was constrained by a set of historical circumstances: the intervention of the RFC and the President in the formulation and execution of policy and the perceived inability to obtain agreement among OMPC members on an appropriate open market policy.

6   Expenditure effects of the 1933 panic

We have every reason to expect that serious expenditure effects accompanied the 1933 panic. In no other panic were banking operations so drastically curtailed. Banking operations were severely restricted in almost every state of the Union. However, the closing of the banks hampered the payments process only temporarily. Ingenuity and business innovativeness provided partial substitutes for checking account payments. How much expenditures on output were reduced or final payment merely delayed or postponed may be discernible in the data available on business conditions.

We attempted to estimate the expenditure effects locally as well as regionally of the 1930 banking crises by extensive use of bank debit data outside New York City. There are, however, no bank debit data available for March 1933 since all of the banks had been closed by presidential decree between March 6 and 13. Therefore, we must resort to alternative aggregate measures of business conditions as reported monthly in the *Federal Reserve Bulletin* and in the *Annual Reports* of the Federal Reserve Board. These measures include industrial production, department store sales, factory employment and payrolls as well as measures of output in particular sectors of the economy, for example, freight carloadings, iron and steel output, and automobile production. Though not always a reliable guide to the behavior of GNP, they do enable us to provide rough estimates of the overall impact of panic.

Table 4.10 shows the behavior of four select indicators of business activity monthly for 1933. Industrial production fell 9 percent between

Table 4.10   *Indices of production, employment, and trade monthly, 1933*
(1923–25 = 100)

1933	Industrial production	Factory employment	Freight car loading	Department store sales
January	65	59	56	60
February	63	59	54	60
March	59	57	50	57
April	66	58	53	67
May	78	61	56	67
June	92	65	60	68
July	100	70	65	70
August	91	73	61	77
September	84	74	60	70
October	76	74	58	70
November	72	72	60	65
December	75	72	62	69

Source: Board of Governors of the Federal Reserve System, *Annual Report of the Federal Reserve Board for 1933*, Washington DC, 1934, pp. 240–1.

January and March; department store sales declined by 8 percent, freight carloadings by 11 percent, and factory employment by 3 percent. All of the indices turned up in April. Industrial production and department store sales were above their levels in January. Factory employment was higher in May than in January. Freight carloadings exceeded the January level in June. The effects of the bank moratoria, state and national, were serious though transitory. Economic activity the rest of the year remained above January levels though not as high as had been attained in July and August. We can conclude that the panic had a temporary observably depressing effect on output and employment. The reopening of the banks signalled the recovery of economic activity.

How much of the decline in output and employment to attribute to bank closings alone and how much to the general depressed state of the economy may be discerned by viewing percentage changes in a variety of indicators of business conditions seasonally adjusted for the January–March 1933 period and the corresponding months of the previous year. Table 4.11 shows percentage changes in the various measures of business conditions for each of the four banking crises of the Great Depression and a separate column for January–March 1932. The last two columns show the behavior of the various measures between January and March 1932 and 1933. The January–March 1933 figures are, with the exception

Table 4.11 *Percentage changes in business conditions measures during four banking crises of the Great Depression plus January–March 1932*

	1	2	3	4	January–March 1932
Industrial production	− 3.5	− 6.1	− 3.9	− 9.0	− 7.0
Manufacturing	− 10.2	− 10.3	− 9.0	− 11.0	− 10.0
Factory employment	− 5.0	− 5.1	− 4.1	− 3.0	− 3.0
Factory payrolls	− 15.3	− 14.7	− 7.8	− 5.0	0
Freight carloadings	− 3.9	− 10.0	− 4.2	− 11.0	− 5.0
Dept. store sales	− 4.5	− 8.3	− 2.3	− 5.0	− 8.0
Iron and steel	− 6.6	− 10.3	− 10.0	− 26.7	− 21.0
Textile	− 4.4	− 29.6	− 11.0	− 12.6	− 8.0
Food products	− 2.1	+ 1.2	+ 4.5	− 4.6	− 11.0
Autos		− 18.0	− 50	− 43.8	− 38.0
Minerals	− 11.4	− 7.8	0	+ 11.0	+ 20.0
Bituminous coal	− 6.3	11.2	+ 5.1	− 10.5	+ 10.0

Source: Board of Governors of the Federal Reserve System, *Annual Report of the Federal Reserve Board*, Washington, DC, 1934, pp. 242–3.

of four indices, almost all uniformly higher than in the first quarter of 1932 when there was no banking panic. But the differences, though larger, were not that much larger than the changes in the corresponding quarter of 1932. They were in fact surprisingly small considering the restrictions on payments by check.

Table 4.11 also shows percentage changes in the various indicators of business conditions during the four separate banking crises of the Great Depression. Although industrial production declined by more in 1933 than in the three previous crises, the decline in manufacturing output was about the same in all four. Factory payrolls for some inexplicable reason declined substantially less in the 1933 panic. There was a sharp contraction in automobile output when the banks closed in 1933, but the decline had been greater during the September–October 1931 crisis. Iron and steel output contracted sharply in 1933. There was a decline in activity in the steel mills from an average of 20 percent of capacity in February to 15 percent in March. Department store sales were the same in January and February 1933 but were substantially smaller in March in areas affected by the suspension of banking operations. Nevertheless, the decline had been greater during the second banking crisis (April–August 1931) and a little less during the first (November 1930–January 1931). The comparison with previous banking crises reveals that the invocation of state and national bank moratoria did not have effects completely out of line with what had happened in the earlier panic periods.

7   Did the 1933 panic resemble pre-1914 panics?

Pre-1914 banking panics reflected the financial organization of the post-Civil War economy. First and foremost is the fact that there was no central bank. The National Banking Act had created a structure of reserve requirements that led to a pyramiding of reserves in Chicago and New York City. Payment of interest on interbank balances induced interior banks to hold large deposits as interbank balances in New York City banks which they employed to make call loans to the stock market. These arrangements made New York City banks highly vulnerable to financial shocks. Shocks to depositor confidence originating in New York were diffused rapidly to the interior as interior banks withdrew their interbank balances. A sudden reduction of funds flowing to the stock market led to spikes in call money rates and a strong response in stock prices. A reduction in the liquidity of New York banks on these occasions placed some banks in jeopardy thereby creating the conditions for a banking crisis. If the shock were serious enough, New York City and interior banks suspended cash payments and arrangements were made by Clearing House Associations to issue Clearing House Certificates.

The chief characteristics of pre-1914 financial panics which emerge from this stylized account are:

1   banking panics, with possibly one exception, had their origins in the central money market;
2   the country's banking reserves were highly concentrated in New York and Chicago banks;
3   during banking panics there were sharp spikes in call money rates and a decrease in stock prices; and
4   there were suspension of cash payments by the banks and the issue of Clearing House Certificates.

The banking panic of 1933, unlike all of the pre-1914 panics with the possibility of only one exception, did not have its origin in the central money market. And there is controversy about whether the 1893 panic had its origin in New York or in the West and the South. Noyes (1909, p. 189) maintained that the bankruptcy of the Philadelphia and Reading Railroad on February 20, 1893 and the failure of the New York Cordage Company on May 5 punctured the bubble of inflated credit and began a "general movement of liquidation." Since 60 percent of the loan expansion of national banks had occurred in the West and the South, he discerned a connection between events in New York and the loss of depositor confidence in the two regions. Sprague (1910, p. 101), on the other hand, saw no relationship between what happened in New York and bank failures elsewhere. He thought that the banking situation in the South was the consequence of real estate speculation, mainly in urban residential property and mineral lands. The Comptroller of the Currency attributed the bank failures to careless and fraudulent management practices and to bank runs.

Nevertheless, irrespective of the origins of the panic both Sprague and Noyes agreed that the uniqueness of the panic resided in the loss of confidence by depositors outside New York City. Sprague (1910, p. 170) stated that not since the establishment of the national banking system had a situation arisen when there was such widespread distrust by depositors in large sections of the country. And Noyes (1909, p. 193) wrote: "no such financial wreck had fallen upon the West since it became a factor in the financial world."

The high incidence of bank failures in the West and the South is revealed in both the annual and monthly figures. Of the 158 national bank suspensions in 1893, 153 were in the West and the South. Nineteen national banks were placed in the hands of receivers between May and June, and the number of state and private bank closings was even greater. Many of the nonnational bank closings were savings banks and private banks in small towns. We conclude, with the possible exception of the 1893 crisis, that the banking panic of 1933 differed from pre-1914 financial panics inasmuch as its origin was outside the central money market.

Those who were responsible for creating the Fed simply ignored the question: How was the Fed supposed to respond to banking disturbances where there was no immediate danger to the central money market? The legacy of post-Civil War panics was that they originated in the central money market and then spread to the rest of the country. Preventing crises in the central money market should, therefore, have been sufficient to ward off national financial crises. No thought had ever been given to what the response of the Fed should be to shocks to depositor confidence originating outside the money market centers and confined largely to banks that were not members of the Federal Reserve System. It was apparently implicitly assumed, without much forethought, that member banks in the interior would have sufficient eligible paper to discount at the Fed, and that nonmember banks would not be a problem.

In another significant detail the 1933 banking panic differed from pre-1914 banking panics. In the earlier period shocks to depositor confidence were always reflected in significant movements in the call money rate. These so called "spikes" in interest rates observed during nineteenth-century financial panics refer specifically to that rate. Sprague (1910, p. 113) stated that stock operators were paying as much as 1/8–1/2 percent per day (45–185 percent per annum) during the 1873 panic; between 3 and 4 percent per day (1,095–1,460 percent per annum) during the 1884 panic. During the 1890 panic call rates were 186 percent per annum.

The spike in the call money rate, however, did not spill over necessarily to other interest rates. While call loan rates were soaring in 1884, rates for mercantile discounts remained practically unchanged at 4 1/2–5 percent. Money market stringency reflected solely the availability of funds to the stock market. The close connection between bankers' balances in New York and call money rates demonstrates how sensitive the stock market was to shocks to depositor confidence. In 1873 stock price volatility was so great that the governing committee closed the Exchange for ten days, an event not repeated in later crises. In 1884 the failure of the brokerage firm of Grant and Ward caused a considerable decline in stock prices. The *Commercial and Financial Chronicle* (May 6, 1893, p. 743) described the stock market crisis that followed the failure of the National Cordage Company "as one of the worst stock panics of short duration that we have ever known in the City."

As a result of fundamental changes in the structure of the banking system, especially the creation of the Federal Reserve System, there was every reason to believe that spikes in the call money rate during financial panics would be eliminated. The nation's banking reserve was no longer concentrated in the hands of New York City banks, and a mechanism had been created for a more flexible supply of reserves. An exodus of bankers' balances from New York need not evoke a sharp response in the call money rate nor should we expect a comparable stock market response. New York banks could replenish their reserve losses by discounting at the Fed and, if the incentive were right, sell bankers' acceptances to the Fed.

As we have shown the interest rate response to the 1933 panic was moderate. The establishment of the Federal Reserve System had introduced important structural changes in how the New York money market behaved and thereby altered expectations about what was supposed to happen during a banking panic. Both the interest rate and the stock market response to a banking crisis were muted by the advent of the Fed.

We also might have expected that the 1914 structural changes would have made obsolete two of the old-fashioned panic remedies – the suspension of cash payments and the issue of Clearing House Certificates. But as we have emphasized repeatedly, there was a reversion to the use of the suspension of cash payments during the 1933 panic. It was unique among US financial panics inasmuch as bank moratoria were used far more extensively to forestall widespread bank insolvencies than in any other financial crisis. Both sound and unsound banks alike were either closed arbitrarily by proclamation of the governors of 48 states or deposit withdrawals were severely limited.

The declaration of a banking holiday in the individual states was neither a remedy for the banking crisis nor a solution to the hoarding problem. It merely postponed the day of reckoning by forestalling further bank insolvencies. Presumably, time might have brought a viable solution, but Hoover was unprepared on his own initiatives to declare a national bank holiday. Hope lay in the new initiatives of the incoming president.

Meanwhile, the effects of the several state bank holidays were to exacerbate hoarding. After restrictions were placed on cash payments, the public hastened to add to its currency holdings in anticipation of further currency restraints. During post-Civil War financial crises Sprague (1910, p. 276) had noted the effects of the suspension of cash payments were to increase "enormously the propensity to hoard money." People were reluctant to deposit cash for fear that banks might not be able to provide currency for future needs. And a suspension of cash payments increased substantially the transactions demand for currency as restrictions on payments with deposits became more widespread. Sprague (1910, p. 68) suggested that the increase in the transactions demand for currency ought not strictly to be characterized as hoarding. It was, nevertheless, a concomitant circumstance of the severity of the restriction placed on currency withdrawals by the declaration of various state banking holidays.

Sprague (1910, p. 68) also identified a third reason for an increase in hoarding during the pre-1914 panics. During a panic currency immediately went to a premium when a suspension of payments was announced. Depositors could profit thereby by withdrawing currency for resale purposes. The premium continued sometimes for as long as thirty days during which time large shipments of currency were made to the interior. The creation of the Fed by providing facilities to increase the note issue eliminated the premium on currency during panics of the Great Depression.

The declaration of the various state banking holidays in February and March 1933 accelerated the amount of domestic hoarding. Uncoordinated individual state action exacerbated the panic. State officials themselves panicked when they observed banking holidays being declared in contiguous states. To conserve the banking assets of their states, they imposed drastic withdrawal restrictions on deposits thereby providing the mechanism for propagating uncertainty and fear to the rest of the nation. The imposition of state banking holidays was the device by which confidence in the national banking system was quickly eroded. Runs, or attempted runs, on all the banks including the soundest were inevitable. Discretionary suspension was not a solution; it was an important part of the problem.

The extent to which pre-1914 remedies for a banking crisis still exercised some influence in 1933 is also revealed by the considerations government and Federal Reserve officials gave to the issue of Clearing House Certificates. As we described earlier, President Hoover recommended on February 14 the issue of Clearing House scrip under the direction of the Federal Reserve banks as a solution to the Detroit banking crisis. But on that occasion Governors Meyer and Harrison of the Federal Reserve objected on the grounds that the issue of scrip would reflect negatively on the "adequacy and flexibility" of the Reserve System!

Adolph Miller, a member of the Federal Reserve Board, suggested on February 24 that the solution to the national banking crisis resided in a bank moratorium and the issue of Clearing House Certificates. According to Hamlin's *Diary* (March 1, 1933, p. 109) the Federal Reserve Board on February 28 discussed thoroughly the issue of Clearing House Certificates but failed to agree on its advisability. Miller brought the subject up again on March 1. Although Hamlin stated that he was prepared to vote with Miller, no further action was taken.

The pre-1914 remedy of suspension of cash payments can be explained quite easily. Bold and courageous leadership was absent. Neither the Fed nor the RFC was willing to accept lender-of-last-resort responsibilities. And the President, though he was fully apprised of the deleterious effects of the gathering storm, was unwilling to act on his own initiative in the declaration of a national banking holiday. Uncoordinated action by the individual states filled the leadership vacuum.

8   The resolution of the banking panic

The depressed state of the banking industry was not fully revealed until after the bank holiday when the government by legislative mandate assumed responsibility for reopening the banks. The Emergency Banking Act of March 9, 1933 granted the government the necessary powers to reopen the banks and to resolve the immediate banking crisis. Only one-half of the nations' banks with 90 percent of the total banking resources were judged capable of resuming business on March 15; these banks were presumably safe which meant that they were solvent. The government guaranteed the soundness of each of the reopened banks. The other half remained unlicensed; 45 percent of these were placed under the direction of "conservators" whose function it was to reorganize the banks for the purpose of eventually restoring all of them to solvency. The remaining 5 percent (about 1,000 banks) would have to be closed permanently.

Draconian measures never employed before nor since were deemed necessary to insure that there would be no revival of panic-like conditions. An officer of the government, the Secretary of the Treasury, was named as sole licensing agent for Federal Reserve member banks. He delegated some of the authority to the Acting Comptroller of the Currency who supervised the national banks and some to the twelve Federal Reserve banks for state-chartered banks. The licensing of nonmember banks was left in the hands of the state supervisory agencies.

The responsibility of the licensing authority was awesome. Whether a bank could be reopened or not depended upon the sole discretion of the Secretary of the Treasury or agents acting in his behalf for member banks. That same authority resided with state banking officials for nonmember banks. There was no time for individual bank examinations. Decisions were made on the basis of whatever information was available at the time which in most cases was bank examiners' reports at the last examination date. Since there were decisions pending to open or not to open 18,000 banks in no more than four days, the task was an especially gruelling one. For a bank to be denied a license to reopen appeared to be on the face of it arbitrary and capricious, particularly since there was no provision for appeal, and the standards of evaluation were not fixed in advance. It would be difficult to conceive of a more arbitrary act of government short of nationalization of the banks. Nevertheless, this action was thought necessary in emergency conditions and received overwhelming support in Congress.

By April 12 the initial licensing program had been completed. Twelve thousand eight hundred and seventeen banks had been licensed to reopen with $31 billion in deposits, broken down, as follows:

	Number	Deposits ($m.)
National	4,789	16.4
State member	636	9.4
Nonmember	7,392	5.0
Total	12,817	30.8

Four thousand two hundred and fifteen banks with deposits of nearly $4 billion did not reopen on that date. By the end of the year 1,105 banks had been placed in liquidation with total deposits of $1.2 billion.

Part of the solution to the crisis resided in eliminating those banks where the hope was small or nonexistent of ever restoring them to solvency. However, an equally important part of the solution was the provision of aid to the reopened banks to insure their soundness. This aid consisted of two kinds: (1) The RFC could purchase the preferred stock of banks – a device to implement their capital – and (2) the Federal Reserve banks could make loans to nonmember banks for one year on good security and could issue Federal Reserve bank notes to insure that currency demands of the public would be fully met.

Post-bank holiday banking policy had as its primary objectives the restoration of depositor confidence, the ending of the banking panic, and fundamental banking reform to restore the banking system to solvency. The Banking Acts of 1933 and 1935 which created the Federal Deposit Insurance Corporation and reorganized the Open Market Committee were aspects of the movement for banking reform touched off by the banking panic of 1933.

The restoration of banking stability was a long drawn out process. In the first stage the immediate task was to restore depositor confidence by encouraging an inflow of currency to the banking system to be accomplished by announcing a definite schedule for the reopening of the banks and assurances that only safe and sound banks would be licensed to do business. Government officials were successful in achieving that goal. The public responded by redepositing hoarded currency in the reopened banks. Between March 13 and March 30 currency in circulation declined by $600 million.

In the second stage provision was made for reorganizing the banks that were allowed to open only on a restricted basis. The RFC played a key role by purchasing the preferred stock and other capital obligations of those banks whose capital had been impaired. RFC purchases of capital obligations including preferred stock are shown in table 4.12.

We can see that RFC disbursements did not assume large proportions before December 1933 most of which went to shore up banks that were attempting to qualify for membership in the Federal Deposit Insurance Corporation. The RFC assumed the task of qualifying as many banks as possible for membership in the FDIC. In October 1933 there were still some 2,300 banks still closed. The importance of the RFC contribution is readily discernible from the fact that by June 30, 1934, it owned 23.6 percent of the capital stock, notes, and debentures of insured banks and the total capital funds of insured banks.

Table 4.12   *RFC purchases of capital obligations: 1st quarter 1933–2nd quarter 1934*

Quarter		($m.)
1st	1933	13
2nd		43
3rd		63
4th		264
1st	1934	594
2nd		817
Total		1,794

Source: Cyril B. Upsham and Edwin Lamke, *Closed and Distressed Banks*, Brookings Institution, Washington DC, 1934, p. 195.

National banks that were insolvent at the time of the bank holiday and were subsequently reorganized sold at least one-half of their new capital obligations to the RFC as did a large number of reorganized state banks. Upsham and Lamke (1934, p. 199) concluded that the provision for an adequate capital structure for reorganized banks "was only made possible by means of RFC aid."

9   Summary and conclusions

The banking panic of 1933 remains an anomaly among US financial panics. A sequence of unexpected shocks to depositor confidence generated by the declaration of bank moratoria by the governors of forty-eight states between February 14 and March 4 brought banking operations to a virtual standstill. Why was it necessary to have resorted to the pre-1914 device of the suspension of cash payments especially after the Federal Reserve System had presumably been created to make suspension of payments obsolete? We have found the answer to that question partly in the confusion about ultimate responsibility for preventing banking crises that existed between the Federal Reserve and the RFC, partly in the RFC's unwillingness to provide the necessary aid to troubled banks in Detroit, partly to the Fed's inability to obtain agreement among the twelve bank governors to pursue a vigorous open market policy, and partly to the President's reluctance to take effective action without the participation of the incoming president. We concluded that a reversion to the pre-1914 device of suspension of cash payment was a failure of effective leadership at the national level. The only recourse short of widespread bank insolvencies was the reluctant assumption of leadership by the governors of the several states. The lack of coordination among the governors of the timing of their actions only exacerbated the panic as depositors rushed to withdraw currency before additional restrictions were imposed.

Depositor behavior was not conditioned solely by solvency of individual banks. There were attempted runs on both sound and unsound banks to obtain cash in anticipation of state banking moratoria.

By the time Roosevelt declared a national banking holiday to begin March 6, the banking system had collapsed. Wigmore and Donaldson have maintained that external, not internal, considerations account for Roosevelt's decision to close the banks. But the gold drain, as we have shown, was not paramount. Banking operations had either ceased or were being conducted at drastically reduced levels in forty-eight states. There was no hope that the governors of those states could resolve banking difficulties on their own initiative when the moratoria ended. The solution rested at the national level, and the first step was to close all the banks and then determine which banks would be allowed to reopen. This was the prescription of the Hoover administration, but lacking the cooperation of Roosevelt was not implemented until his inauguration.

The story of the 1933 crisis is a story about the confusion of responsibility between the Fed and the RFC, personality clashes between Senator Couzens of Michigan and Henry Ford over aid to the Detroit banks, and a perception of RFC officials that binding legal constraints prevented them from avoiding the closing of all Michigan banks. It was a financial debacle that was allowed to occur for want of a few million dollars!

Table A4.1 *Federal Reserve notes in circulation weekly by district, not seasonally adjusted, December 31, 1932 to April 5, 1933 ($m.)*

	Boston	New York	Philadelphia	Cleveland	Richmond	Atlanta	Chicago	St. Louis	Minneapolis	Kansas City	Dallas	San Francisco	Total
1932													
Dec. 31	196	588	238	285	102	97	692	104	81	90	39	227	2,739
1933													
Jan. 4	196	584	235	285	101	98	694	104	82	91	39	229	2,738
Jan. 11	191	562	231	282	99	97	686	105	81	90	38	225	2,688
Jan. 18	187	556	230	278	97	97	685	137	81	91	37	221	2,697
Jan. 25	185	545	228	277	97	98	692	134	81	93	36	240	2,706
Feb. 1	187	557	232	276	97	98	696	133	82	98	36	238	2,730
Feb. 8	187	562	235	279	98	98	706	134	84	100	36	241	2,773
Feb. 15	188	593	244	301	100	111	748	136	86	101	36	247	2,891
Feb. 21	193	610	253	306	106	110	803	137	89	103	36	252	3,000
Feb. 28	216	798	288	383	156	112	920	153	95	113	43	287	3,580
March 8	243	970	300	423	196	127	1,113	174	113	148	55	321	4,215
March 15	264	995	309	424	214	158	1,068	174	117	150	58	344	4,292
March 29	243	848	277	368	187	177	960	156	102	127	44	280	3,748
April 5	240	824	268	355	182	154	930	152	102	125	43	174	3,644

Source: Commercial and Financial Chronicle, weekly from December 31, 1932 to April 5, 1933.

5   Banking crises of the Great Depression: a reassessment

We set out initially to reconstruct each of the four banking crises of the Great Depression. That task is now completed. What remains to be done is to extract from that account what we have learned, if anything, about the banking crises of the Great Depression. Did these crises differ from pre-1914 banking panics? And, if they did, how did they differ? Did panic-induced failures in the early 1930s differ from the nonpanic-induced suspensions in the twenties? Did panic-induced failures cause output to vary? And, finally, what was the response of the Federal Reserve to accelerated bank closings between 1930 and 1933? We have the knowledge and experience of four separate banking crises with which to attempt to answer these important questions.

Our description and analysis of the first three crises revealed that decomposition by Federal Reserve District disclosed wide geographical disparities in the incidence of bank suspensions and hoarding. So much so that we concluded that the 1930 banking crisis and the April–August 1931 crisis were region specific. These two crises were not nationwide in scope, and the expenditure effects associated with the 1930 crisis were minimal.

Unlike pre-1914 panics, the "eye" of the banking disturbance was not the New York money market. The establishment of the Federal Reserve System in 1914 had altered the response of the New York money market in at least two important ways: the short-term interest rate response was muted, and strong stock market reactions were eliminated. There was in contemporary economic jargon "a change in regime" which had the effect of altering permanently expectations about how the central money market would react to unanticipated financial shocks. Whatever questions remain about the success of interest rate smoothing inaugurated by the Federal Reserve, the Fed did eliminate the sharp spikes in the call money rate observable in all pre-1914 financial crises.

151

The geographical incidence of the banking crises

One of the chief contributions of this study has been to increase our knowledge and understanding of what happened in each crisis at the microeconomic level. Aggregate data on bank suspensions, deposits in failed banks, and currency hoarding obscure, and quite possibly distort, what was going on at the local and regional level. Since the history of nineteenth-century panics is a history of events in the excited New York money market, the neglect of local and regional effects was, perhaps, understandable. But such neglect cannot be justified for the banking crises of the Great Depression which had their origins somewhere in the interior of the country, not in New York.

Serious gaps in our knowledge still exist, especially about the course of banking panics in primarily rural areas. But we have been able to identify successfully clusters of urban bank closings that account for a sizeable share of bank suspensions and deposits in suspended banks in both the 1930 and 1931 crises thereby eliminating the geographical vagueness that is the inevitable result of relying solely on financial aggregates.

Locating the source or sources of banking disturbances is a two stage procedure. In the first, we located where the incidence of bank suspensions and currency hoarding was the highest either by state or by Federal Reserve District, and, in the second, we attempted to identify which banks failed and in which cities.

We discovered that there was a high concentration of bank suspensions, deposits in failed banks, and currency hoarding in a relatively small number of Federal Reserve Districts that figured in more than one banking crisis. Chicago, for example, played a prominent role in the first three banking disturbances. Chicago, Pittsburgh, and Philadelphia were centers of crises during the accelerated bank suspensions between April and August and September and October 1931. The principal findings to emerge from the evidence on the incidence of bank failures are, as follows:

1 During the banking crisis of 1930 two out of every five bank closings were located in the St. Louis District attributable to the banking disturbance created by the collapse of Caldwell and Company. Chicago was not even a close second with only 15 percent. Four Districts accounted for 80 percent of total bank suspensions and slightly over one-half of the deposits of failed banks. One-half of the Districts had fewer than 10 percent of the suspensions.

2 Between April and August 1931 one-third of all bank suspensions were in the Chicago District. There was a mini panic in the city of

Chicago in June and a full scale panic in Toledo in August. The Cleveland Federal Reserve District had two-thirds of the deposits of suspended banks. However, in six Districts there was little or no change in currency hoarding.

3   During the September–October crisis in 1931 three Districts – Chicago, Cleveland, and Philadelphia – accounted for two-thirds of the deposits of suspended banks and one-half of the increase in hoarding, the same percentage for the three Districts in the April–August crisis. Moreover, there was a high concentration of failed banks in only three cities – Pittsburgh, Philadelphia, and Chicago.

The first two banking crises can best be characterized as region specific inasmuch as at least one-half of the Districts had either fewer than 10 percent of bank closings (1930) or there was little or no change in hoarding (April–August 1931). There was not a uniform response across the twelve Federal Reserve Districts whether measured by the incidence of bank suspensions or the loss of depositor confidence. But, regrettably, we do not know how this experience differed from the pre-1914 panics. We know little or nothing about exactly what happened in the interior of the country during pre-1914 panics. Sprague's (1910) classic study – *History of Crises Under the National Banking System* – contains occasional references to bank suspensions in the interior but nothing that would allow us to measure and compare their impact regionally.

We also learned that the September–October 1931 crisis did not conform fully to conventional views of a banking panic; that is, there was no indiscriminate run on banks by depositors whose confidence had been shattered. Bank runs in Chicago, Pittsburgh, and Philadelphia were directed against particular banks that were known to be weak and that were located in certain specific sections of the city. There were no indiscriminate runs on the largest banks in the central city.

Neither the number of bank suspensions nor deposits in suspended banks captures what was happening during the 1933 panic. The declaration of bank moratoria by the individual states arbitrarily closed or severely restricted deposit withdrawals throughout each state. By the end of the day on March 4 bank moratoria were in effect in all forty-eight states. A national banking holiday declared by Roosevelt did not go into effect until March 6.

The 1933 panic was idiosyncratic. In no other financial panic was there such a widespread use of the device of the bank holiday. The declaration of bank holidays by individual states was the mechanism through which depositor confidence in surrounding states was seriously impaired.

Governors of the several states "panicked" and sought bank holidays and restrictions on deposit withdrawals.

Nothing perplexed Federal Reserve officials more than the shift in the geographical source of banking crises from the New York money market to the interior of the country. Historically, banking panics had been a phenomena of central money markets. By eliminating disturbances in the New York money market, banking panics would disappear, or so Federal Reserve policymakers reasoned. When this did not happen, they sought an explanation which stressed that the accelerated bank suspensions in 1930 and 1931 were a sequence of isolated "local" responses and deserving of a "local" response as well; that is, the responsibility for doing something about banking disturbances in troubled areas resided with the Federal Reserve Bank in the affected District when the source of unrest was a member bank. Whatever the merits of their view, historical experience did not provide comparable episodes by which to guide their conduct.

Did the banking crises of the Great Depression differ from pre-1914 panics?

Calomiris and Gorton (1991, pp. 114–15) have conjectured that the panics during the Great Depression "appear to be of a different character than earlier panics." And they gave three reasons for the alleged differences: (1) during the Great Depression panics did not occur near the peak of the business cycle; (2) they resulted in widespread failures and losses to depositors; and (3) the Federal Reserve played a "pernicious" role in the banking collapse of the 1930s. Unwise central banking policy was more responsible for what happened to the banks than inherent instability of the banking system.

Evidence does not support the claim that the timing of the banking crises of the Great Depression differed all that much from pre-1914 panics. Table 5.1 shows National Bureau of Economic Research business cycle troughs, peaks, and panic dates from 1873 through 1933. In five of the six cycles with panics, the panic occurred during the contraction phase of the cycle. In only two of the six cycles did the panic occur near the peak: in 1873 the panic preceded the downturn by one month, and in 1893 the panic followed the downturn by one month. There is, of course, an element of arbitrariness in dating cycle peaks and troughs, but I would not describe the panics of 1884, 1890, and 1907 as having occurred after a cyclical peak. The contraction phase lasted ten months in the 1890 cycle and thirteen months in the 1907 cycle. The panics in each instance occurred around the midpoint of the contraction, not near the cyclical

Table 5.1   *NBER reference cycle peaks, panic dates, time preceding and time succeeding a peak, 1873–1907 (NBER business cycle reference dates)*

Peak	Trough	Panic date	Time proceeding peak (months)	Time succeeding peak (months)
October 1873	March 1879	September 1873	1	
March 1882	May 1885	May 1884		17
March 1887		April 1888		
July 1890	May 1891	November 1890		4
January 1893	June 1894	February 1893		1
December 1895				
June 1899				
September 1902				
May 1907	June 1908	October 1907		5
August 1929 ·	March 1933	October–November 1930		19
		September–October 1931		
		February–March 1933		

Source: Sherman Maisel, *Macroeconomics*, 1982, New York, W.W. Norton, p.290.

peak. The 1884 panic also occurred around the mid point of the contraction phase; the contraction phase lasted thirty-eight months.

The use of the term "pernicious" scarcely does full justice to the Fed's total response to the banking crises of the Great Depression considering that the Fed prevented the monetary base from contracting during the 1930 and 1931 episodes, and the New York money market remained stable.

Our analysis of the banking crises of the Great Depression has revealed the following set of discriminating characteristics:

1   Unlike pre-1914 panics, there were multiple banking crises during the contraction phase from 1929 to 1933, at least two of which were region specific.
2   The "eye" of the crisis was no longer the New York money market.
3   At least two of the insidious effects of pre-1914 crises were eliminated: spikes in the call money rate and serious stock market upheavals.
4   Unlike pre-1914 banking panics, there was greater elasticity of the currency supply in response to the increased demands of the public. Federal Reserve notes in circulation expanded substantially in each of the four banking crises.

What is especially noteworthy about the Great Depression experience is not that the banking crisis did not occur near cyclical peaks as suggested by Calomiris and Gorton, but the fact that there were multiple crises or panics during 1929–33 which clearly marks off the banking panics of the Great Depression from all previous post-Civil War experience. Nor was the contraction phase of the 1929–33 especially long (forty-three months). The contraction lasted sixty-five months from October 1873 to March 1879 and thirty-eight months from March 1882 to May 1885. The 1933 panic occurred at the cyclical trough thereby distinguishing it from all prior panics.

The significance of multiple crises resides in the fact that there was a progressive and continual deterioration of depositor confidence as revealed by the monthly data on currency in circulation seasonally adjusted. In neither 1930 nor 1931 did the ending of the banking crisis result in a large return flow of currency. Deceleration of bank suspensions and deposits in failed banks was not followed by dishoarding as in previous pre-1914 panics. During the 1930 and 1931 crises hoarding accelerated during the panic, leveled off at a higher plateau and then resumed its upward thrust, except in 1933. Post-banking holiday government intervention restored depositor confidence and was immediately followed by a $1 billion inflow of currency.

Each successive wave of bank suspensions before 1933 led to a further deterioration of depositor confidence and reduced the liquidity of the banking system, thereby contributing to the weakness of thousands of commercial banks. In a very real sense the panics of 1930 and 1931 never ended, if we mean that the ending of the panic implies a restoration of depositor confidence manifest by a return flow of currency to the banking system.

Another distinguishing feature of the multicrises of the Great Depression is the fundamental change in the center of the initial disturbance. Unlike pre-1914 panics, the "eye" of the crisis was no longer the New York money market. In earlier panics, the initial shock originated in the New York market with reverberations extending outward to the rest of the country. A description of what happened in New York was regarded as tantamount to a description of the panic. During the Great Depression, the initial shock originated generally in the interior without observable effects in the New York money market.

The establishment of the Federal Reserve System in 1914 eliminated crises in the central money market. Although there were some bank failures in New York City – especially the failure of the Bank of United States in December 1930, there was no panic. Before 1914 there were a few mechanisms for increasing the supply of bank reserves to money market center banks such as gold imports and a redistribution of US

Treasury balances. After 1914 there were basic changes in the reserve supply mechanism that gave the money center banks access to the reserves of the newly created Federal Reserve banks. This radically altered the money market response during a financial crisis. The short-term interest rate response was thereby muted and serious stock market disturbances entirely eliminated. In fashionable economic jargon, there was a "regime change" which altered expectations about how the central money market responded to a financial shock. We have demonstrated that all of the banking crises of the Great Depression originated in the interior of the country with urban bank suspensions playing a prominent role. Nashville, Little Rock, Memphis, Louisville, Charlotte, and Chicago were the centers of the banking crisis in 1930. The eye shifted to Pittsburgh, Philadelphia, and Chicago in 1931 and to Detroit in 1933. In 1931 the very largest banks escaped unscathed, the major damage was confined to the cities' peripheries and outlying areas and especially to saving banks and trust companies that were heavily invested in real estate. We have explained why we do not feel that the failure of the Bank of United States in New York City does not belong in this list. To describe what was happening within the cities in 1931, we coined the phrase "mini panics" to reflect what was going on and to emphasize that there was no indiscriminate run on all banks regardless of size within the city.

To the Fed's everlasting credit is the fact that it prevented panic in the New York money market. No matter how serious bank suspensions were in the rest of the country, they were not a source of disturbance in the central money market. Maintaining stability in the New York money market was a top priority of Federal Reserve policymakers. The Fed was also successful in preventing a decline in the monetary base during the 1930 and 1931 banking crises. A necessary but not sufficient condition for preventing a decline in the money stock is the stability of the monetary base; it was the inflexible supply of bank reserves and the currency supply that led to monetary reform and the establishment of the Federal Reserve in 1913. The machinery of the Act enabled the Fed to avoid a sharp contraction of reserves in the central money market.

Three characteristics emerge from an examination of the behavior of currency in circulation during banking crises of the Great Depression: (1) total currency in circulation increased as a proportion of the total money stock however defined; (2) the ratio of Federal Reserve notes to total currency in circulation increased discernibly during the course of each banking crisis, and (3) the ratio of large denominational currency to total currency in circulation markedly increased during the three banking disturbances.

The ratio of Federal Reserve notes to total currency in circulation increased from 32 percent immediately before to the banking crisis of 1930 and to 60 percent at the peak of the 1933 panic. The ratio increased perceptibly in each of the three banking crises: 3.7 percentage points in 1930, 5.1 percentage points in 1931, and 10.4 percentage points in 1933. Part of the explanation for the increase resides in the behavior of large denominational currency (Federal Reserve notes of $50 and above). In each of the three banking crises the share of large denominational currency markedly increased: 3.2 percentage points in 1930, 2.3 percentage points in 1931, and 4.1 percentage points in 1933. Contrary to the expectations of the founders of the Fed, the provision of an elastic supply of currency was not sufficient to halt banking panics.

Traditional wisdom notwithstanding, we have shown that the Fed's discount rate response to the gold drain in October 1931 played no causal role in initiating the banking crisis. Fully 60 percent of the increase in domestic currency hoarding took place between September 16 and October 7 before the New York Fed raised the discount rate. Moreover, we have shown that arguments to the effect that the Fed should have offset increases in the currency–deposit ratio are anachronistic. Knowledge of how the currency–deposit ratio affected the money stock was not available before the path-breaking contributions of Angell and Ficek in 1933 and Meade in 1934.

President Hoover's initiatives in creating the National Credit Corporation (NCC) on October 4, 1931 in the middle of the banking crisis obfuscated the lender-of-last-resort responsibilities of the Fed by placing Eugene Meyer, Governor of the Federal Reserve Board, as also Chairman of the new agency. There is a very thin line between the division of responsibilities for preventing bank failures and forestalling banking panics. The Fed remained on the sidelines while the successor to the NCC in 1932 the Reconstruction Finance Corporation (RFC) was engaged in making loans to individual troubled banks that were solvent, both member and nonmember banks. The Fed's perception of its role as lender-of-last-resort was conditioned by what it regarded as a binding legal constraint, that is, its inability to lend to nonmember banks. Hoover deliberately created the NCC and the RFC to fill that gap. The RFC, however, never assumed the lender-of-last-resort responsibilities abdicated by the Fed.

One of the more serious policy errors of Fed officials was its inability to muster internal support for a program of liberal purchases of government securities in an effort, not as Friedman and Schwartz would have it to prevent a decline in the money stock, but, given the lack of knowledge of the determinants of the money stock, to restore depositor confidence and a return flow of currency to the banking system. Policymakers were well-informed about the magnitude of currency hoarding and that the ending of the banking crises in both 1930 and 1931 did not signal an expected return flow of currency to the banks. The restoration of depositor confidence required a demonstration of Federal Reserve leadership by a bold stroke such as liberal purchases of securities. The sooner the better. By 1932 when the Fed did initiate a program of substantial purchases, it was abandoned too soon because of a failure to understand the build up of excess reserves.

Did bank failures cause the Great Depression?

Friedman and Schwartz (1963) discovered the banking crisis of 1930 and elevated it to the status of a national banking panic with causal significance for explaining why a relatively mild recession turned into a depression in the Fall of 1930. They found the origin of the 1930 crisis in the New York money market, that is, in the failure of the Bank of United States. There was, however, no panic in that market. They claimed that the failure of the Bank of United States in December 1930 by its very size and prestigious name generated a loss of depositor confidence nation-wide, an increase in hoarding, and accelerated bank suspensions and deposit losses in failed banks. By failing to identify the banking panic in November resulting from the collapse of the Nashville investment banking house of Caldwell and Company they attributed the loss of depositor confidence solely to the closing of BUS. It seems clear from the evidence on the incidence of currency hoarding that the increase of hoarding in December occurred in those same Federal Reserve Districts that had absorbed the effects of the failure of Caldwell and Company. The November shock was still exerting delayed effects on the number of bank suspensions and deposits in failed banks in the St. Louis, Richmond, and Atlanta Districts.

We have identified two channels through which panic-generated bank suspensions may have affected output adversely: (1) Friedman and Schwartz's money stock channel, and (2) Bernanke's bank credit channel. We were not able to isolate significant national expenditure effects in either of the first two banking panics as predicted by Friedman and Schwartz's money stock channel. And Bernanke made no effort to discriminate between panic and nonpanic related episodes in estimating the significance of the bank credit channel.

Ferderer and Zalewski (1994) have identified a third channel in addition to the money stock and bank credit channels through which the banking panics of the 1930s may have contributed to the severity of the

Great Depression. In their view the banking crises of 1931–33 increased interest rate uncertainty which, in turn, adversely affected national investment spending. They constructed a measure of interest rate uncertainty by attempting to isolate the risk premium embedded in the term structure of interest rates. The estimated risk premium moved along a strong upward path between 1929 and 1933 with some acceleration during each bank-panic episode. The increase itself was quite small, not much more than three to six basic points in each panic. Nevertheless, they maintained that even such small changes provided important information about the behavior of interest rate uncertainty. The strong upward thrust in the risk premium was the result of bank failures and the collapse of the international gold standard, the largest increase having occurred in 1932 when there was no nationwide banking panic. Banking panics per se were not the most important source of the increase in the risk premium though they played a contributing role.

If the banking crisis of 1930 has economic significance, it resides in showing that the spate of bank failures was independent of the behavior of interest rates and income. And the historical and econometric evidence does not speak with one voice on this matter. The historical evidence is consistent with the view that the regional panic generated by the failure of Caldwell and Company was an autonomous disturbance generated by questionable managerial and financial shenanigans inaugurated in the twenties to foster growth and expansion and unrelated to current developments. If the historical evidence is credible, and I think that it is, causation should go from bank failures to income. The econometric evidence gives conflicting interpretations of the causal role of bank failures: Boughton and Wicker (1984), Anderson and Butkiewicz (1980), and Trescott (1992) agree that bank failures were an important determinant of the money stock but disagree about the role of interest rates and income. The jury is still out.

The first banking crisis looms large in the Friedman and Schwartz interpretation of why the recession turned into a major depression in the final months of 1930. Bank failures in 1931 were attributed to the impairment of the market value of bank assets brought on by the persistent decline in economic activity, especially to the depreciation of bond prices. But we have not been able to uncover any evidence that would directly link bank suspensions and the depreciation of bond prices for the September–October 1931 banking crisis. As we have reported, bond depreciation was a primary cause of bank suspensions in only six out of 105 closed banks sampled by a Special Committee appointed by the Federal Reserve Board in 1930. Nor is there any evidence that falling bond prices contributed to bank suspensions in the state of Arkansas in

1931. Granted the available evidence leaves something to be desired. Nevertheless, what little that there is fails to support the hypothesis that bank failures in 1931 were attributable to bond depreciation. More work needs to be done to resolve this issue.

The role of gold during the banking panics

We have not been able to discover any negative role that gold played in either the first (1930) or second banking panics of the Great Depression. It was totally irrelevant in the first and a source of strength in the second. Due mainly to financial disturbances in Europe, gold imports amounted to $300 million between April and August 1931. The Fed responded by reducing the buying rate and acceptances allegedly to aid Britain in protecting her gold reserve. The effect of the importation of gold was favorable inasmuch as it tended to offset the internal drain.

Gold did not emerge as a potential source of disturbance before September 1931 when Britain abandoned gold. The onset of the panic coincided with the British announcement; it had nothing to do with the Fed's increase in the discount rate in October. Having said that, we have not been able to uncover any evidence that would tie increased bank suspensions and hoarding directly to the external drain. Uncertainty about future gold convertibility may have prompted the public to test the solvency of US banks, but we cannot be certain. One might have thought that such uncertainty would first manifest itself in the central money market among sophisticated investors. But that did not happen. Bank suspensions were concentrated in Pittsburgh, Philadelphia, and Chicago and not among the larger banks. Depositor unrest in those three cities can not be traced to gold convertibility considerations.

The external drain in March 1933 was substantial. The Federal Reserve Bank of New York came dangerously close to suspending gold payments. Nevertheless, the banking crisis during the last two weeks of February was motivated more by the indiscriminate and uncoordinated declaration of banking holidays by state governors than by gold convertibility considerations; however, it cannot be determined that depositor confidence may have been affected by fears that gold payment was threatened.

Our conclusion is that gold outflows played a secondary role in causing the banking panics of the Great Depression with the possible exception of the September–October 1931 panic. Although the onset of the gold outflow is coincident with the increase in hoarding and bank suspensions, much work remains to be done on establishing a statistically significant relationship.

Causes of bank suspensions: random withdrawals or asset shocks?

In chapter 1 we identified two rival theories of banking panics: the random withdrawal and the asymmetric information hypotheses. The random withdrawal hypothesis attributes bank suspensions to bank illiquidity induced by a contagion of fear. The asymmetric information approach assigns a key role to bank insolvency induced by asset shocks due to weak management, fraud and malfeasance, or persistent adverse economic conditions countrywide or in a particular sector. This classification does not preclude that both may be at work simultaneously.

The failure of the regional investment banking house of Caldwell and Company in November 1930 is consistent with the random withdrawal hypothesis. Calomiris and Gorton (1991, p.149) state specifically that the random withdrawal approach sees "the greatest threat to banks coming from regionally concentrated shocks transmitted through the correspondent network." The Caldwell collapse, as we have described it, was a region specific exogenous shock which generated a run on affiliated banks in at least four states; the relationship was not primarily a correspondent network in the narrow sense, rather it included 120 affiliated banks that were connected by a chain banking system as well as by a bank holding company. General depositor unrest spread to unaffiliated banks in the three Federal Reserve Districts most directly affected: St. Louis, Atlanta, and Richmond.

Calomiris and Gorton rejected the random withdrawal hypothesis as an explanation of pre-1914 banking panics from the evidence accumulated by the Comptroller of the Currency giving the cause of individual national bank closures around bank panic dates in the pre-1914 era. The Comptroller identified only one national bank whose demise he attributed to the bank run. Calomiris and Gorton concluded that panic-related suspensions must have been unimportant! What they failed to notice, however, was that the Comptroller's Report distinguished between banks that suspended temporarily and later reopened and banks that failed; that is, banks that went into receivership. The tables in the Comptroller's Report for 1893 (pp. 180–91) which list causes of bank failures do not include the large number of banks that suspended and later reopened, the class from which we would expect contagion of fear and bank runs would have played a crucial role.

I (Wicker, 1995) have estimated that during the 1893 panic an average of over 40 percent of the banks in the six cities where the panic was the most intense and holding two-fifths of the deposits of suspended banks were solvent at the time of the suspension. These are, to my knowledge, the first estimates for any banking panic revealing the extent to which frightened depositors exhibited their loss of confidence in both solvent and insolvent banks during a bank run.

Saunders and Wilson (March 1993) found significant contagion effects for a sample of national bank failures for the period of 1930–2, but their study does not discriminate between bank suspensions during panic and nonpanic months. They consider bank failures over the year as a whole. They compare net deposit withdrawals for *ex ante* "good" banks with "bad" banks. Since *ex ante* good banks suffered increased deposit withdrawals as well, they argue that the evidence is consistent with a contagion effect. But deposit withdrawals need not be associated with bank runs. Deposit contraction may be associated with changes in the monetary base or changes in the currency–deposit and reserve–deposit ratios.

White (1984) could find little support for the bank illiquidity view of bank suspensions during the 1930 panic. He concluded that the bank failure experience during the 1930 crisis did not differ from that of the 1920s when there was no general loss of depositor confidence. He compared the ninety-six national banks that failed between November, 1930 and January, 1931 with a stratified random sample of nonfailing banks with similar assets from the same cities and local areas in the three previous years. The statistical model he used to explain failures was a logit regression with independent variable that included: total capital accounts to assets, cash items to total deposits, US government bonds to assets, loans and discounts to assets, and total deposits to assets. Using likelihood ratio tests he performed pairwise tests for all pairs of years and found: "Although the tests are not conclusive, they do support the view that the characteristics of bank failures did not change drastically between 1927 and 1930. The 1930 crisis was not a departure from the 1920s experience."

White's econometric evidence appears to conflict with our microhistory evidence which revealed widespread bank runs and bank illiquidity. Can these two apparently different explanations of bank suspensions during the 1930 panic be reconciled?

One possible explanation for the discrepancy may be that national banks that failed between November 1930 and January 1931 had different characteristics from those specifically identified in the microhistory narrative. But included in White's list of ninety-six failed banks are approximately sixty-seven failures in the Federal Reserve Districts of Saint Louis (40), Atlanta (14), and Richmond (13). These suspensions in the three Federal Reserve Districts account for 60 percent of the total number of bank suspensions. All of the bank suspensions in these Districts were not induced by illiquidity and runs on banks. But we do know that a high proportion were, especially in November and December. I see no reason for thinking that the national banks that failed during the crisis in these three Districts were not subject to the same depositor uncertainly and runs as the other banks.

A second explanation of the discrepancy may be that the characteristics of national banks may have differed from characteristics of nonnational banks that failed and that were not included in White's sample, a consideration he duly noted.

A third possible explanation of the conflicting testimony of the evidence is that White's regression equations do not include an independent variable that proxies for bank runs. An important variable may have been omitted. Currency hoarding may serve as a proxy for runs on banks; that is, currency hoarding by Federal Reserve District. The conflicting evidence remains a puzzle and requires further consideration.

Thies and Gerlowski (1993) have attempted unsuccessfully to confirm White's hypothesis that bank failures of the 1930s were caused by the more fundamental problem of insolvency rather than panic-induced illiquidity. Their use of data pooled by three-year periods from 1931 to 1932 can be faulted as an inappropriate period for testing. To test the hypothesis about the cause of bank suspensions during banking crisis, the data that are relevant pertain to the actual months of the banking disturbance not to nonpanic-related months as well. Pooling the data by three year periods ignores the distinction between those months during which the panic was rampant and nonpanic months. Of course, the relevant crisis episodes include only ten of the thirty-six months between 1930 and 1932 when 38 percent of total bank suspensions occurred. Moreover, White was careful to point out that his results applied solely to the panic-related crisis months in 1930. He did not deny that illiquidity played a significant role in subsequent bank failures in 1931 and 1932.

The conclusions to which we are inevitably drawn by our study of the banking crises of the Great Depression are that they differed from pre-1914 panics in their origins, in the central money market's response, and in the choice of available remedies. The sole exception was the banking panic of 1933 when there was a reversion to the pre-1914 device of the suspension of cash payments but in a different guise – the declaration of statewide banking moratoria.

The historical evidence lends strong support to the view that the origin of the 1930 crisis was an exogenous shock whose influence was region specific with minimal expenditure effects outside the affected region. Interpretations of the econometric evidence remain highly ambiguous offering neither firm support nor a clear rejection of the causal role of bank failures in contributing to the contraction of output.

Furthermore, reassessment of Federal Reserve conduct during the five banking crises is called for in the light of our findings; failure to have responded to an increase in the currency–deposit ratio was not due to ineptness but rather to the lack of knowledge available at the time on the determinants of the money stock multiplier; the Fed's discount rate increase in October 1931 played no causal role in initiating the banking crisis; and the Fed was successful in maintaining stability in the New York money market. That, however, does not exonerate Fed officials who were unwilling to support a vigorous program of open market operations in 1930 and 1931 for the explicit purpose of restoring depositor confidence and reducing the amount of hoarding.

References

Newspapers

Chicago Tribune
Commercial and Financial Chronicle
Detroit Free Press
Indianapolis News
Kansas City, Kansas Gazette
Louisville Courier Journal
New York Times
Omaha Daily Bee
Omaha Morning World – Herald
Philadelphia Inquirer
Philadelphia Record
Pittsburgh Post Gazette
St. Louis Post Dispatch
Toledo Blade
Wall Street Journal

Books and articles

Anderson, B. and Butkiewicz, J. 1980. "Money, Spending, and the Great Depression." *Southern Economic Journal* 47 (October): 388–403.

Andrew, A.P. 1908. "Substitutes for Cash in the Panic of 1907." *Quarterly Journal of Economics* 22 (August): 497–516.

Angell, J.H. and Ficek, K.F. 1933. "The Expansion of Bank Credit." *Journal of Political Economy* 41 (February): 1–32,
1933. "The Expansion of Bank Credit II." *Journal of Political Economy* 41 (April): 152–93.

Balke, N.S. and Gordon, R.J. 1989. "The Estimation of Prewar Gross National Product: Methodology and New Evidence." *Journal of Political Economy* 97 (February): 38–92.

Ballantine, A.A. 1948. "When All the Banks Closed." *Harvard Business Review* 26 (March): 129–43.

Barro, R. 1977. "Unanticipated Money, Growth, and Unemployment in the United States." *American Economic Review* 67 (March): 101–15.

Bernanke, B.S. 1983. "Nonmonetary Effects of the Financial Crisis in the Propagation of the Great Depression." *American Economic Review* 73 (June): 257–76.

Board of Governors of the Federal Reserve System. 1933. "Bank Suspension in the United States, 1892–1931," vol. V. Mimeo, Washington DC.

   1934. *Annual Report of the Federal Reserve Board for 1933*, Washington DC.

   1941. *Banking Studies*. Baltimore: Waverly Press.

   1943. *Banking and Monetary Statistics, 1914–1941*, Washington DC.

   1976. *Banking and Monetary Statistics: 1914–1942*. Washington DC.

   (various dates). *Federal Reserve Bulletin*, Washington DC.

Boughton, J. and Wicker, E. 1979. "The Behavior of the Currency-Deposit Ratio During the Great Depression." *Journal of Money, Credit and Banking* 11 (November): 405–18.

   1984. "A Reply to Trescott." *Journal of Money, Credit and Banking* 16 (August): 336–7.

Calomiris, C.W. and Gorton, G. 1991. "The Origin of Banking Panics: Models, Facts, and Bank Regulations." *Financial Markets and Financial Crises*, edited by R. Glenn Hubbard. Chicago: University of Chicago Press, pp. 109–73.

Calomiris, C.W. and Mason, J.R. 1994. "Contagion and Bank Failures During the Depression: The June 1932 Chicago Banking Panic," unpublished paper, Champaign, Illinois.

Chari, V.V. and Jagannathan R. 1988. "Banking Panics, Information, and Rational Expectations Equilibrium." *Journal of Finance* 43 (July): 749–60.

Comptroller of the Currency. 1893. *Annual Report*. Washington DC: Government Printing Press.

Diamond, D. and Dybvig, P. 1983. "Bank Runs, Liquidity, and Deposit Insurance." *Journal of Political Economy* 91 (June): 401–19.

Donaldson, R.G. 1992. "Sources of Panics." *Journal of Monetary Economics* 20 (November): 276–305.

Eichengreen, B. 1992. *Golden Fetters*. New York: Oxford University Press.

Esbitt, M. 1986. "Bank Portfolios and Bank Failures During the Great Depression: Chicago." *Journal of European History* 46 (June): 455–62.

Ferderer, J.P. and Zalewski, D.A. 1994. "Uncertainty as a Propagating Force in the Great Depression." *Journal of Economic History* 54 (December): 825–49.

Friedman, M., 1974. "Anti-Semitism and the Great Depression." *Newsweek*: 90 (November 16).

Friedman, M. and Schwartz, A.J. 1963. *A Monetary History of the United States, 1867–1960*. New York: National Bureau of Economic Research.

   1986. "The Failure of the Bank of the United States: A Reappraisal: A Reply." *Exploration in Economic History* 23 (April): 199–204.

Garlock, F.L. and Gile, B.M. 1935. *Bank Failures in Arkansas*. Bulletin No. 315, Agricultural Experiment Station, University of Arkansas, College of Agriculture (March): 17–19.

Goldschmidt, Raymond. 1933. The *Changing Structure of American Banking*. London: Routledge.

Gorton, Gary. 1987. "Bank Suspensions and Convertibility." *Journal of Monetary Economics* 15 (March): 177–93.

Hamilton, D. 1985. "The Causes of the Banking Panic of 1930, Another View." *Journal of Southern History* 51 (November): 581–608.

Hamlin, C.S. *Diaries*. Library of Congress. Washington DC.

Harrison, George L. *Papers*. Butler Library, Columbia University.

"Discussion Notes," Minutes of the Meetings of the Board of Directors of the New York Federal Reserve Bank. G.L. Harrison Papers. Butler Library, Columbia University.

1932. *Creation of a Reconstructive Finance Corporation*: *Hearings Before a Subcommittee of the Committee on Banking and Currency*. US Senate. 72nd Congress, 1st Session.

Humphrey, T.M. 1987. "The Theory of Multiple Expansion of Deposits: What it Is and Whence it Came." *Economic Review*. Federal Reserve Bank of Richmond 73 (March–April): 3–11.

Jacklin, C. and Bhattacharya, S. 1988. "Distinguishing Panics and Information-Based Bank Runs: Welfare Policy Implications." *Journal of Political Economy* 96 (June): 568–92.

James, F.C. 1939. *The Growth of Chicago Banks*. Vol. II. New York: Harper and Brothers.

Kennedy, S.E. 1973. *The Banking Crisis of 1933*. Lexington: Kentucky University Press.

Lucia, J. 1985. "The Failure of the Bank of United States: A Reappraisal." *Exploration in Economic History* 22 (October): 402–16.

Maisel, Sherman. 1982. *Macroeconomics*. New York: W.W. Norton.

McFerrin, J.B. 1969. *Caldwell and Company*. Nashville: Vanderbilt University Press, originally published by the University of North Carolina Press in 1939.

Meade, J. 1934. "The Amount of Money and the Banking System." *Economic Journal* 44 (March): 77–83.

Mills, O. 1932. *Creation of a Reconstructive Finance Corporation: Hearings Before a Subcommittee of the Committee on Banking and Currency*, US Senate, 72nd Congress, 1st Session.

1934. Minutes of the Board of Directors of Reconstruction Finance Corporation, February 22, 1933 as quoted in *Stock Exchange Practices: Hearings* 73rd Congress, 2nd Session, Part 10.

Noyes, A. 1909. *Forty Years of American Finance*. New York: G.P. Putnam's Sons.

O'Brien, P. 1992. "The Failure of the Bank of United States: A Defense of Joseph Lucia." *Journal of Money, Credit and Banking* 24 (August): 374–84.

Olson, J.S. 1977. *Herbert Hoover and the Reconstruction Finance Corporation*, Ames, Iowa: Iowa State University Press.

Open Market Policy Conference. 1931. "Executive Committee Minutes." October 26, 1931. Federal Reserve Board Records: Washington DC.

Rand-McNally Bankers' Directory. 1931. Rand McNally: Chicago.

Report of Study Commission for Indian Financial Institiutions. 1932. Indiana-polis: Wm. B. Burford Printing Company.

Romer, C. 1986. "Spurious Volatility in Historical Unemployment Data." *Journal of Political Economy* 94 (February): 1–37.

1988. "World War I and the Post-War Depression: A Reinterpretation Based on Alternative Estimates of GNP." *Journal of Monetary Economics* 22 (July): 91–115.

1989. "The Prewar Business Cycle Reconsidered: New Estimates of Gross National Product, 1869–1908." *Journal of Political Economy* 97 (February): 1–37.

Saunders, A. and Wilson, B. 1993. "Contagious Bank Runs: Evidence From the 1929–1933 Period." Mimeo. New York University Salomon Center.

Schwartz, A. 1981. "Understanding 1929–1933." *The Great Depression Revisited,* edited by K. Brunner. Boston: Martinus Nijhoff, pp. 5–48.

Schweikart, L. 1995. "A New Perspective on George Wingfield and Nevada Banking, 1920–1933." *Money and Banking: The American Experience,* Fairfax, Virginia, George Mason University Press, pp. 325–42.

Sprague, O.M.W. 1910. *History of Crises Under the National Banking System,* Washington DC: Government Printing Office.

Standard Statistical Base Book Bulletin. 1932 and 1934. Standard Trade and Security Services, Statistical Section.

Stevens, E. 1934. Testimony Before Committee on Banking and Currency. US Senate on *Stock Exchange Practices.* 73rd Congress, 2nd Session, Wa-shington DC: Government Printing Office.

Sullivan, L. 1936. *Prelude to Panic.* Washington DC: Statesman Press.

Temin, P. 1976. *Did Monetary Forces Cause the Great Depression?* New York: W.W. Norton.

1990. *Lessons From the Great Depression,* Cambridge, Mass.: MIT Press.

Thies, C. and Gerlowski, D. 1993. "Bank Capital and Bank Failure, 1921–1932: Testing the White Hypothesis." *Journal of Economic History* 53 (December): 908–14.

Trescott, P.B. 1984. "The Behavior of the Currency–Deposit Ratio during the Great Depression." *Journal of Money, Credit and Banking* 16 (August): 362–5.

1992. "The Failure of the Bank of United States, 1930." *Journal of Money, Credit and Banking* 24 (August): 384–99.

Upham, C.B. and Lamke, E. 1934. *Closed and Distressed Banks,* Washington DC: The Brookings Institution.

US Department of Commerce. *Survey of Current Business* various dates. Washington DC: Government Printing Office.

Vickers, R.B. 1994. *Panic in Paradise, Florida's Banking Crisis of 1926.* Tuscaloosa: University of Alabama Press.

Wheelock, D. Private Correspondence.

White, E. 1984. "A Reinterpretation of the Banking Crisis of 1930." *Journal of Economic History* 44 (March): 119–38.

Wicker, E. 1966. *Federal Reserve Monetary Policy 1917–1933*. New York: Random House.

    1995. "The Banking Panic of 1893." Unpublished paper. Bloomington, Indiana.

    1980. "A Reconsideration of the Causes of the Banking Panic of 1930." *Journal of Economic History* 40 (September): 571–83.

    1982. "Interest Rate and Expenditure Effects of the Banking Panic of 1930." *Explorations in Economic History* 19 (July): 435–45.

Wigmore, B.A. 1985. *The Crash and Its Aftermath*. Westport, Conn.: Greenwood Press.

    1987. "Was the Bank Holiday of 1933 a Run on the Dollar Rather than the Banks?" *Journal of Economic History* 47 (September): 739–56.

Willis, H.P. and Chapman, J.M. 1934. *The Banking Situation*. New York: Columbia University Press.

Young, O. 1931. "George L. Harrison Papers," Discussion Notes. Butler Library, Columbia University.

Young, R., 1931. Minutes Open Market Policy Conference, August 16. George L. Harrison Papers. Butler Library, Columbia University.

Index